GIANTS IN THE ROUGH

JERRY LOUT

"If you ever wondered what it would be like to be a missionary in Africa, this compelling narrative is a must read. From encounters with evil forces and spitting cobras to co-laboring alongside some of God's choicest servants. I highly recommend this book." Bill Sherman, Tulsa World editor (ret)
Bill Sherman. Tulsa World editor 35 years (ret)

Jerry's life story of following Jesus "with a limp" is a true inspiration to me and many other people like me. In *Giants in the Rough* Jerry gives us a winsome and intimate look into the remarkable stories and people that have shaped his story and, as a result, have given us a hopeful and challenging example to follow. Thank you, Jerry, for sharing it with us!
Gyle Smith, Pastor. Believers Church, Tulsa, OK

Jerry writes from a place of both profound humility and passionate love for Jesus and the lost. The reader will be entertained by whimsical stories of family life in a foreign land. But beware - it is impossible to escape being provoked by Jerry's devotion and insights. His message is communicated through the ancient gift of story-telling blended with the wisdom of a seasoned elder in the Father's family. I highly recommend this book
Tim Way. Church planter/Leadership trainer

Through these vignettes of his life, Jerry Lout walks us through his call and life as a missionary in East Africa. The stories, sometimes funny, sometimes challenging, sometimes encouraging, sometimes difficult, reveal his humble spirit and open heart. Through them Jerry shares how his God led, taught, trained and used he and Ann in marvelous ways, not only among the Africans whom he loved, but the missionaries with whom he served. I highly recommend "Giants in the Rough". There are lessons in it for us all.

Tom Brazell. Global Ministries Director, Elim Fellowship (ret)

I first met Jerry Lout when I was an International graduate student at the University of Tulsa and he served as director of International Student Ministries. His story is one of obedience and dedication to serve, a story of a human with limitations, reliant on a gentle Savior and His grace. This book will encourage you, give you occasional chuckles, but most importantly, will inspire you.

Lara Adedokun. Healthcare Consultant

When someone opens their life and their heart, we should pay attention. Having known him personally, I can attest to Jerry Lout's very very big heart. He carries a limp, but his love towards others does not. His openness inspires.

Paulette McNeal. Bukuria Mission. Kenya. Bible Teacher

Jerry Lout is a genuine follower of the Lord Jesus Christ. His writings provide for the reader a true-to-life learning experience. Having observed the author's life up close, I happily commend him and the valuable lessons you will find in these pages.

Ron Meyers. Director of Missions, Oral Roberts University (ret)

This book is exciting, hard and easy, a page turner, and just wonderful. I highly recommend it.

Anna Joy Parker, granddaughter, Leonard Coote, Founder I.B.C.

GIANTS IN THE ROUGH

Editor: RJ Thesman
Book Design: Rick Magley
Photography: UM Photography

Where conversations are introduced, the author has sought to remain true to
narratives as they occurred. My thanks to readers extending grace where
precise accuracies may be unclear.
For the sake of anonymity, some names are changed.

Printed in the United States of America
First Printing, 2019

ISBN-13: 978.1096875482
ISBN-10: 1096875482

TO
Christ-followers everywhere
who, hearing his "Go and make disciples"
yield themselves in loving response,
"Here I am. Send me"

THANKS TO

Writing Coach and Editor RJ Thesman, whose exceptional skills and counsel aided greatly in bringing about GIANTS' successful completion

Cover Design illustrator Rick Magley, bringing rare artistic gifts into play. Offering up quality reflections of a truly majestic continent

Jim Lassiter, investing hour on hour of finely-honed skills in the organizational and publishing process – marked by patience, talent and good humor

Millard Parrish, bringing keen-eyed focus to the proofreading craft employed in service under Christ, reflecting a large-hearted devotion to the peoples of Africa

My wife Ann, for patiently enduring my hermit lifestyle at a keyboard in the room at the end of the hall

CONTENTS

PROLOGUE

Kilimanjaro's towering image held us spellbound. From our home in her foothills, my thoughts give rise to faces and names of fellow pilgrims about the region. Indeed, wherever messengers of Christ have borne his presence to this world. Imperfect spokesmen, many in search of steadier footing as if navigating Kili's own steep terrain. No strangers to hardship, they pressed on, embodying an old phrase, "nothing comes to Spring, save through Winter." Their mission -- a call of a carpenter -- "Go, make disciples of all nations."

Humbled in the company of sacrificial warriors, we bear witness to them, their enduring imprint on Africa's spiritual landscape. Giants in the rough.

Chapter One

TWISTS AND TURNS

I GRIMACED. *A couple more steps and you're in,* I goaded myself. It was my first-ever visit to a chiropractic clinic – this detour on my way to Africa.

I nudged the door. My face contorted as I shuffled through to the foyer.

One thing was clear. . . though I had long-discarded my pair of crutches from the polio bouts, those limping days of childhood were hardly my last.

Halting steps moved me toward a check-in counter. At it sat a prim, middle-aged woman. Another pain shot across my lower back. My knees buckled and I caught myself, barely averting a crash to the hardwood floor. The lady took charge.

"Oh! Here, right here, sir!" Quickly moving my way, she indicated a straight-back chair. I eased into it, arching my back at odd angles.

"The doctor will see you in just a minute," she offered with a sympathetic smile.

Another slow turn in the chair. Perspiration beaded my forehead. Thanking the receptionist, I accepted a pen and *first-visit* patient form. After a couple entries, I relaxed and reviewed the incident that brought me to this cottage-turned-clinic in the Alamo city.

A wry smile visited my lips.

If Francis could see me now.

Shortly before our San Antonio move for Bible college, my co-worker at Tulsa's North American Aviation asked what job awaited me beyond the state line. Between winces now, I imagined his "I-told-you-so." If he could only see me in this bone-cruncher establishment.

Well, Francis, it's like this. Down at the corner of Caldera and Bandera there's this Phillips 66 station. . . .

Midafternoon yesterday I had grabbed two car tires, both attached to their heavy rims. Lifting a weighty load while swiveling about defied good judgment, a fact shouted to me via a stab near my waist line.

Mercifully, within an hour of my clinic visit, relief broke through. I moved to the parking lot without a whimper, the bone-cruncher profession winning my devotion.

This early encounter in our South Texas move served as a preview for my wife Ann and me, our pathways ahead, their twists and turns, challenging episodes, comforting break-throughs. The adventure was underway.

We would grapple with mysteries, get confronted by cultures, religious and otherwise.

But first, some needed training.

◊◊◊

How do you turn a Pentecostal into a Baptist, then to some ill-defined other, while retaining qualities of them all?

A fellow-student with the middle name "Worthy" crossed my path.

"Hi, Brother Jerry! Say, I've been wanting to see you. Got a minute?"

David Worthy Mulford flashed his broad, tilted smile. A rich smile, conveying an easy warmth.

By school tradition, each new freshman class came up with its distinct label. I was ten years David's junior and counted among the Lively Stones. David reigned as president of the Illuminators.

I parked my hard-bound theology text and the equally dense Thompson Chain Bible by the sidewalk. A jumble of protruding scribbled notes flapped as a gust tried to part them from the oversized books.

David launched in. "Jerry, would you and Ann like to join Betty and me in pastoring a church the other side of town?"

I was intrigued. David, my fellow Pentecostal, read my questioning gaze. Then he dropped the 'B' word.

"Eastwood Baptist asked me to be their fill-in pastor till they find a replacement for the fellow that left. The church was saddled with a bunch of debt through the sale of bogus bonds. The error of a past leader. The people are hurting. Although it's a sad situation, maybe this could be the Lord opening a door for us to bring some encouragement.

"Also, you and I could gain experience preaching, teaching and, you know, church work in general."

Ann and I prayed. Deciding that experience itself factored into any education, we thanked the Mulfords and plunged in.

The early weeks convinced me that leading songs for Eastwood Baptist came easier than teaching New Testament to adults twice my age. But Paul's ancient letter to believers in a Mediterranean seaport grew on me, "Brothers and sisters, let's open our Bibles to the book of Ephesians."

Chapter Two

IDENTITY CRISIS

"ALL ABOARD!"

At an instructor's promptings, weekends found a ragtag band of college students venturing to practice street preaching downtown. One Sunday evening left me conflicted.

A neatly-groomed young man had paused on the boulevard sidewalk to take in the accordion music. Then a team member preached, assailing all passersby with a volley of repent-and-get-saved appeals. The sermonette ended and the young man approached.

"Excuse me", he offered, "could I ask a question?" I nodded.

"Why are you guys so cynical?"

Cynical? What did that mean?

Lacking depth to answer well, I turned defensive.

"No, we're not cynical. We're just trying to show people the way to. . . ."

My lame defense trailed off. When the polite gent realized

I had nothing more, he quietly moved down the street. The brief encounter left me wondering, and a little troubled.

Exploring later the meaning of cynical, "a disbelief in the sincerity of motives", I puzzled over it. *Can I find ways of sharing my faith other than just lobbing gospel missiles at passersby?*

That day on Houston Avenue moved me to seek help beyond myself. How might things have gone if the gent and I had sat together, shared a thoughtful visit over life and its meaning. Might God have been present there too, announcing his good news?

Street evangelism - Open-air campaigns - Stadium events. Historically, such outreaches, I realized, had seen spiritual orphans, limping in their lostness, gathered into God's family by the droves. May such good practices endure. Yet may a different kind of question from thoughtful seekers grow more common: *"Why are you guys so caring?"*

When self-conscious limping brings insecure feelings, I'm tempted to shield myself, maybe adopt an artificial label.

Like non-sectarian.

I relish good memories of my childhood church, where the underside of wooden benches supplied a landing place for well-spent chewing gum.

One day I studied an odd word on the church's signboard, practiced sounding it out before knowing its meaning: Non-sec-tar-ian.

The bold word, a statement declaring our religious identity, held a prominent space on the sign. Printed large, it displayed itself just beneath another label, Non-Denominational.

It seemed important to us that visitors knew we were a different kind of church. Quite different. If I had been old enough, I might have puzzled, *why would a good community as ours feel a need to announce we were unlike others?*

The sign provided me an early sampling of complicated words. Later, I discovered others, like "oxymoron."

I started noting in believers, myself included, troubling leanings toward independence. Like the church sign, we prefer to stand alone. Even when standing alone means barely staying upright at all.

Over time I grappled with the fact that religion, like politics, finds splintering an easy thing. We separate, forming new, more-distinctive camps. It happens despite us, despite the fact that common beliefs may be more common than we realize.

Is it because erecting walls demands less energy than building bridges? When I lay half-paralyzed in a polio ward, I preferred the mattress over the therapy room.

My broader world of college life pressed me to face my own *sectarian* attitude. Of labeling inferior or less righteous, that gathering of the faithful the other side of town or those just down the street. A personal non-sectarian sign, fashioned by myself, adorned a wall in my inner corridor. It brought me face to face with my interior limping.

To our surprise, Ann and I found our on-ramp into the world of Christian service flavored by complementing, rather than competing, camps. This shift grew over time. Baptists and Pentecostals – polar-opposites in expression and style – rejoiced together, celebrated, even generously gave. Faith became a living concept far bigger than any of us dreamed. We realized how distinctive camps of Christians – regardless the label – could suffer limps. Yet could find the heart to move past handicaps like divisiveness.

A.W. Tozer* suggests we're best off tuning our hearts to Jesus. "Has it ever occurred to you that one hundred pianos all tuned to the same fork are automatically tuned to each other? They are of one accord by being tuned, not to each other, but to another standard to which each one must individually bow. . . ."

Along our infant-steps toward ministry we grew humbled and heartened. We encountered curious cross-breeds along the way. A hand of greeting from one believer to another, a twinkle of mischievous warmth lighting their eyes. One smiles, "I call myself a Bapticostal."

Chapter Three

FACEOFF

A NEWSPAPER POSTED me to their teletype division. I said goodbye to my gas station job.

How about this! Coming to work right across the street from the Alamo. If Davy Crocket and Jim Bowie could only see the San Antonio Express casting her shadow over their fortress. Shading my eyes against the Texas sun, I lifted my gaze.

The News plant stretched upward a full eight stories, matching my hometown's all-time highest structure, the Commerce Building. In child-hood I couldn't have dreamed I would one day work in such a skyscraper. I little imagined *now* what I would soon witness, and what news my tele-typing fingers would relay from inside this place. A heart-stopping feat in human history, fulfillment of a young president's outlandish prediction.

But for now, in a modest library atop a Texas hill, I would survey the history of another kind of president: founder and past head of my Bible school of choice.

◊◊◊

The ambitious Brit puzzled his dilemma.

"If I'm to make my case that the book my good landlord calls *holy* is no more than a fanciful collection of tales and contradictions, I suppose I must fetch myself a copy." His musing was brief. "By Jove, I shall!"

Young and self-assured Leonard Coote had known just where he was headed in life. Endowed with a keen mind and an appetite for adventure, Leonard arranged to sail from his native England for the islands of Japan. "Seize the moment,", came the rallying cry. "Now is the time . . . Japanese business markets are ripe . . . Venture forth, your fortune awaits!"

Signing on with a Liverpool firm spearheading business in eastern lands, he boarded a ship. Other young Englishmen had blazed impressive trails, making it big, finding their fortunes.

But a worry nagged Leonard.

Those who had *not* done well were distracted by hard drink and party-going. Many, it was noted, wound up addicted, sidelined, chasing another bottle to blunt the pain of derailed dreams.

Resourceful Leonard crafted a strategy. *I shall find living quarters somewhere safe, of better surroundings than those poor blokes settled for.* The scheme had led him to the man with the holy book.

"Yes", the resident missionary offered, "we can make our spare room available and you're welcome to join us for mealtimes." They quickly settled on a room-and-board fee and sealed the agreement with a handshake.

Not long after moving in, Leonard challenged the Bible teacher on his faith and the validity of the Scriptures. But, the missionary smiled and politely declined. "I'm happy sharing my story and what the Bible means to me. But debate. . . argue the matter? No, I'm not your person for that."

This frustrated Leonard, bringing him to his dilemma and to his decision.

Arriving home one evening, he carried in his satchel a fresh-bought Bible. With a pen and a clean ledger added to his arsenal, Leonard smiled. "There! All that remains now is to read through it, registering its errors as I go. We *will* have that discussion, the missionary and I, and I shall be ready."

What the young man did not factor in was a bold, terse phrase lying within the ancient text. Nothing could have prepared Leonard for the moment.

"Splendid dining," Leonard smiled at the missionary's wife. "I'm a lucky chap, finding this place for my lodging." Nodding to the family, he excused himself.

Entering his room, he gave his body a good stretch. Moving the few steps to his desk, he took up the ledger he had bought. Squiggles on an open page revealed his latest entries. Markings showed his focused quest to prove the clergyman wrong. To expose the holy book for what it was — a bundle of contradictory myths.

He reached for the Bible. Fingering the book marker, he flipped to the page last visited.

Over past weeks his practice had become ritual: Arrive home from a day's work, down a cup of tea, tidy up a bit, join the family for dinner, retire to his room and resume the task at hand.

His daily regimen with the Bible had taken Leonard deep into the Old Testament. He had moved beyond the Wisdom books, jotting notes as he read. All of Prophet Isaiah's sixty-six chapters brought the sum of his readings to twenty-three books.

The book of Jeremiah lay open at chapter seventeen. Leonard came to verse nine, "The heart is deceitful above all things, and desperately wicked: who can know it?"

Leonard Coote was drawn in. He read it once more. And was undone.

Chapter Four

COURSE CORRECTION

THE PROPHET'S words broke over him like a great wave suddenly deluging a child at play. One moment all is serene. All is chaos the next.

Tears surged upward from a bottled place deep inside, like a long-capped reservoir straining for release. Anguish — an all-encompassing sorrow with a depth he had never known.

Those fourteen words wrecked him. The first line looped in his mind again and again. *"The heart is deceitful above all things."*

Self-assurance stripped by a bold, piercing statement. He tried quieting his sobs. He felt the worst kind of pain, detecting his own dreadfulness, the deception of his heart. Shame.

Leonard knew he had travelled a road of self-deception. He read the final words. *". . .And desperately wicked: who can know it?"*

The anguish remained, even stronger, crashing like waves.

"Deceitful *and* wicked." His sense of guilt brought him to

the floor. Weeping, he lay prostrate. His sense of unworthiness pressed him further. Moving a throw rug aside he lay face-down on the bare surface. Finally, he slept, though not at peace.

The next day came and went. Then the next. When not at work or trying to sleep, he lay on the floor. Leonard knew his misery had a name. Sin. Years later he would recount the scene in his memoir, *Impossibilities Become Challenges*.

"I saw myself as I had never seen myself before. Lost, undone, wicked. It seemed as if my very clothes smelt of the awfulness of sin." In his drive to dismantle this holy book, the book was dismantling him. In a single verse the Bible exposed him, shining its light on his pride.

Entering his third day of misery, Leonard thought to exit his room, find a place in the back yard and go face-down to the bare earth. Then. . . "Something arrested and stilled my mind."

Leonard "saw" an image of a cross, possibly a vision. Affixed to the cross with iron nails was a bleeding savior.

"I seemed to understand this blood was for my sins." He knew the man to be Jesus. "He was saying to me, 'I died in this way for you. I shed my blood for your sins. Just accept my work of redemption.'

"I did so, crying out, 'I believe. I believe.'"

◊◊◊

Altering a life's course needs more time and space for some than for others. The Willis Brothers made popular a truck-driver song, *Give me Forty Acres and I'll turn this Rig Around*. For others, like Leonard Coote, change seems immediate — a one-eighty turn. Certainly, there would come tweaks, adjustments of behavior and attitude as life moved past his initial conversion. Still, the term "radical" fit Leonard's shift. And peace — rich and undeniable — displaced the turmoil of his past.

Leonard felt genuinely reborn. "Joy flooded my being as I realized I was now a child of God. Everything was different. The very leaves on the trees the next morning had a different tint. . . ."

Love for God fired a new passion within as he wasted no time sharing the news. "I must carry the message to the Japanese."

Sending off for Japanese language pamphlets, Leonard handed them out at markets and street corners. Prayer, Scripture, Community, Worship — each discipline anchored him. Fulfilling his five-year commitment to the company that brought him to Japan, he chose to remain. God added another missionary to his Far East force.

Bible school years strengthened my conviction to work overseas. Hallelujah Hill's library drew me in. Its volumes of stirring narratives recounted the passions and labors of men and women yielding themselves to service. Like America's first missionary, Adoniram Judson who with his wife and at huge personal cost, sailed to Burma. Then the five young men speared to death by tribesmen of Ecuador as they sought to bring Christ's message to jungle people.

With his zeal for training, Leonard Coote launched Bible schools in Japan and Korea before moving to America. In Texas, he founded the International Bible College (IBC) in 1942. Leonard coined an inspiring phrase from the school's initials: *Impossibilities Become Challenges*

Chapter Five

BLUEGRASS BENEFACTOR

WE STARTED GIVING Mrs. Hottenstein a Sunday morning lift to Eastwood Baptist. Mrs. H's many years as a Kentucky-mountain school teacher had formed her. A few months in, she broached a topic she had grappled with. Peering at me through steel-rimmed lenses, her words direct, "I want you to do something."

At ninety years and counting Mrs. H's spunk had not waned. The spindly but keenly-postured schoolmarm was dead serious.

"I need you and Ann to bring me details of your employment earnings, along with your overall monthly budget." She did not pause to note our reactions. She had our attention.

"I need to know your living expenses, tuition and other school-related fees, transportation and so forth—whatever counts as routine costs." The retired lecturer wasn't finished. Long stretches navigating Kentucky hill classrooms had clearly forged an aura of authority. She leveled her vision.

"Jerry, the truth is you are spending far too much time working a job down at that paper. You need to give more hours doing what you came to this place to do. To give yourself to the class time required, to your assignments, exam preparations and the like." The aged voice shifted tone for the first time in her monologue, a softer tenor.

"I want to help. I will do my part to cut your hours at that downtown newspaper. You can arrange with them to work a lighter schedule. I'm sure they'll work with you." She knew no such thing but that was beside the point. "I will help make up the difference."

Our car slowed. "Ah, here we are. Thank you once again for your kindness, giving me the ride."

I walked her up three steps and onto her porch, my hand lightly at her elbow. She stepped inside and turned, facing me. From beyond the screen it was obvious her eyes had resurrected that piercing gaze.

"Remember now. Next week. Have it ready." Crisp. Determined.

I responded in a tone that may have matched my youngster voice of long ago. "Yes, ma'am, I'll do that. I promise."

Mrs. Hottenstein's gesture did achieve what she hoped, freeing me for my college work. And the extra hours away from the teletype keys meant added time with my nurse-student wife. Our two ships-passing-in-the-night rested a few added minutes each day in our common harbor, the thirty-five-by-eight house trailer we called home.

The added margin also freed me to drive northward one week. To a meeting I felt curiously drawn to visit.

"Hey David, I'm heading up to my home church in Oklahoma for some meetings they're having next week. If you're free, it would be great if you could come along."

The nine-hour road trip brought us to the doors of *Living Way Tabernacle*. What followed in the coming minutes set the stage for decades of adventure.

Vigorous hand-clapping joined robust singing as organist Ragsdale's nimble fingers brought his instrument to life. Monday night marked the first in a string of special meetings, and the sanctuary had nearly filled. David and I found seats near the back.

Rev. G.C., a preacher hailing from the deep south, was handed the mic. He was a near giant by any standard I knew. It was preaching time.

Over the past weeks my thoughts had pivoted back and forth between two topics regarding our Africa call. A language spoken there whose tones I could not recognize. And a phrase. . . *leadership training*. A seemingly random visit with a new acquaintance from abroad had spawned reflections. The two themes would not let go.

Swahili. Leadership training.

Rev. G. C.'s deep, graveled voice thundered as he plunged further into his message. Rivulets of sweat glistened on his broad face as his three hundred pounds of Georgia preacherman paced across the front. Up and down the center aisle. His command of the sacred text was impressive. His passion ran deep.

Twenty minutes into the sermon it happened.

Chapter Six

VITAL SIGNS

G.C. STRODE up the center aisle. Suddenly, in mid-sentence he halted. His head tilted upward. An unusual pause. Then the preacher-man voiced a single word no one expected, certainly not me.

"Swahili!"

I gawked his direction, taken by the sudden turn in his message, especially by that word. *Swahili.*

I felt a mist of tears form, the hint of a gathering stream. The preacher's tone softened, repeating that word. "I'm hearing Swahili spoken." He scanned the audience.

"God has called someone in this room to go as a missionary to east or central Africa."

Another pause, longer this time. I felt compelled to move. Rising from my seat near my mentor-friend, David, my response felt surreal.

As I moved toward the altar, each step added to the emotion. An odd blend of feeling, somber excitement, stirred inside me. Meanwhile, the giant clergyman with the southern drawl found his own stride. He spanned the half-church distance between us. Rev. G.C.'s great open hand stretched forward in pursuit of my skull-top. An old-fashioned word of Pentecostal prophecy seemed imminent.

"Son," the Reverend solemnly announced, "God has called you to be his servant."

The weight of the words settled over me like a commissioning charge. Then followed another word, a further echo from my past-days musings. "God has called you to serve African leaders by training them in God's law, so they walk in his Word and they teach others also."

The message settled, somewhere in my inner core. In that moment, nothing could erode my conviction, my sense of assurance. If anything had ever felt a sure thing, I knew this was it. I, we—Ann and I — were affirmed in our calling. To a place and a people neither of us had direct knowledge of. Only that Africa was the place and Swahili most likely the language.

Awash in tears, I found my way back to the seat. The weeping kept on but softer, leaving me only vaguely mindful of the church service. And of its sudden new direction. What?

An unscripted church offering was underway. For air fares. To Africa.

The preacher-man had shifted from prophesying mode to Holy Ghost fund-raising. I sat quiet, marinating in a fog of wonder. A tender, loving presence enshrouded me.

Rev. G.C. drew a bill from his wallet and waved it to the gathering, sounding a challenge. "Who will join me tonight in getting this young man and his wife over to Africa. . . so they can start doing God's work?"

A circular collection basket found its way to the preacher's side. In moments it overflowed. This special week of meetings had not been billed as a missions' conference, yet everyone present was suddenly taken by a get-the-gospel-into-the-world passion. Unfettered generosity, cash gifts and pledged offerings flowed to the basket up front. Once the tally was made, enough had come in to fully cover two air tickets to a far-off land.

Africa, here we come. Oh my.

The Oklahoma road trip with its surprise turn of events ended. David and I headed back to San Antonio.

"Brother Jerry," David's easy drawl interrupted the silence as the car hummed southward. "Hasn't this trip been just something? Imagine what Ann's going to say."

Whatever my wife might end up voicing, I was surely not ready for what David himself would soon say.

Sunday came and Eastwood's worship service was underway. A couple of late arrivals settled into their pews. Pastor David, smiling his tilted smile, stood at the podium.

"You know, dear folks, our Lord is an amazing God." David eased into the topic of our Oklahoma visit. Poised at my usual spot on the platform, I mentally rehearsed a hymn I would guide the worshipers in. Then I caught a mention of my name.

Oh, my goodness. . . Is he going to have me tell these very baptisty Baptists about the big Georgia preacher-man? About the prophecy in Okmulgee and the Holy Ghost offering? Oh my.

Smiling broadly and with a gesture, David turned my way. ". . . And so, I'd like Brother Jerry to come and share something of what God did at that meeting."

Stepping forward, I surveyed the gathering. Dear folks, precious families Ann and I had worshiped with and had grown fond of sat quietly, clearly eager to hear what I would share. Realizing how closely we had grown, my anxiety faded.

Words came easily. No persuasive tone was needed. I sensed their understanding. They welcomed and celebrated the news of God's working in Ann's and my life. All in their attentive Baptist way.

To our amazement God seemed to be setting things in motion. Ann's precocious childhood forecast, "When I grow up, I'm going to be a missionary in Africa" neared fulfillment with each passing day.

I passed the mic back to David, moved again to my seat and took up the song book. My underside had barely warmed the church bench when Pastor David's appeal grabbed my attention.

Yet another offering?

"Folks, I feel the Lord wants us to get in on this missionary adventure with Brother Jerry and Sister Ann." David paused. "The Louts will need a car once they're in Africa, right? Let's trust God to let Eastwood get them that car. What do you say?"

For a church with sparse revenue, the guy at the pulpit had thrown a big challenge. I could not have dreamed the coming surprise.

Like ripples on a pond, smiles spread through the gathering. Heads nodded. Once more, I sat befuddled while a community of common believers dug deep. And once more, joyously, without constraint.

Reaching for cash, a check book, a scrap of paper to indicate a faith-promise offering, our precious Eastwood friends rallied. The collection of funds passed as promptly as it began, and the service transitioned.

Following our customary after-service mingling, Ann and I crossed the gravel lot to our vehicle. The head-spinning week had flown, and we needed to catch our breath, find some time together.

The crunch of parking lot gravel behind us. David's quick-paced sprint toward our direction. "Hey guys," he blurted, his face glowing. Presenting us with a note, figures scribbled up and down, our pastor-friend smiled, "Maybe this will help you move around once you get there. It's the car offering."

Stunned was too tame a word. What an outpouring from a congregation of such humble size and means. I read aloud, "One thousand eight hundred dollars."

We could only shake our heads. "Wow! Thanks, Lord!"

On a balmy June day in Nairobi, the keys of a spanking new Volkswagen Beetle jingled in my hands. The Kenya shillings purchase price marked on the bill of sale equaled one thousand, eight hundred U.S. dollars.

Chapter Seven

MEET THE PRESIDENT

"Yes, this is Art Dodzweit. Can I help you?" Thus, began our entry into a decades-long journey among a distinctive breed of people. Missionaries.

It came on the heels of a class assignment in Church History.

Reverend Jensen, portly and congenial, spelled out our task in steady, methodical tones, "On each of your desks you see a list of names: church denominations, missions agencies, Bible schools. You are to select one. Write a short letter to their office, requesting a copy of their by-laws. Then complete a type-written report." His steady monotone continued, ". . . Who they are, when they incorporated, something of their vision. Turn it in by the end of the month."

Scanning the long list of organizations, I planted a finger on a line mid-way down. My research-project was underway.

David spotted me soon after and we launched our conversation about overseas plans. The topic shifted to missionary-sending organizations or agencies.

"You know, Brother Jerry, it was a long time ago, but my

father used to teach at a place called Elim Bible Institute. The school's linked to an agency, Elim Missionary Assemblies. I think they do a lot of work in Africa. You might contact them."

"Hmm, where's the agency located?"

"Elim is in New York."

"Lima, New York?"

"That's right. Yes." He sent a questioning look.

"I just sent a letter to those folks asking for a copy of their by-laws."

"Wow! What are the odds?"

We could only laugh.

An info packet postmarked New York reached our Texas mailbox. Submitting my assignment, Ann and I pondered the random happenings. Turning to her I asked, "Shall we call Elim?"

"Yes, let's call Elim."

My first-ever phone call to New York brought me in touch with the pioneer missionary now visiting California.

Art Dodzweit suggested I speak directly with Elim Missionary Assembly's president. My second New York call set in motion a journey we would not forget.

"This is Carlton Spencer."

"Sir, I'm calling from San Antonio, Texas. My wife and I hope to serve in Africa."

"San Antonio, you say? How interesting."

Why interesting? Another coincidence brewing?

Spencer went on, "I'll be in your city in a few days. In fact, I'm speaking at your school's chapel."

Interesting indeed.

◊◊◊

"So! *This* is the man with the black heart."

Wednesday chapel ended and the guest speaker found his way from the platform to my row. His greeting wasn't quite what I expected, especially coming from an esteemed ministry head.

He seized my shoulders and studied my face, then smothered me in a strong bear hug. He thumped my back as if suddenly running into an old friend. A rich shock of silver-white hair complimented his mouthful of gleaming teeth. Instantly I liked him, this Carlton Spencer, Elim Missionary Assemblies president.

The black heart. . . what an amusing, yet tender link to hearts moved for a dark-skinned people.

We felt good about pursuing an Africa-minded group. While IBC strongly championed missions, its vision centered on Far East lands and on Mexico, a short hop from the Alamo City. A long weekend into our third year had found us and fellow students, dust-laden, mesmerized, immersed in Mexican culture. The school's traditional Easter outreach south of the border invigorated our hearts for missions.

Welcomed now as missionary candidates, our stride toward Africa picked up pace. Ann's training brought her to Licensed Practical Nurse status as my IBC commencement drew near.

Chapter Eight

HILLTOP STROLL

A SPRINGTIME SAN ANTONIO breeze caressed IBC's *Hallelujah Hill* as I strolled about her dome. I savored memories, taking in this view of which I never tired. A myriad of twinkling city lights stretched far to the southeast. My reflective mood wakened images —faces and scenes of recent years. We would soon move from this place. Distant Africa felt suddenly less distant.

What had I specially treasured along the way, about and atop this hill? Highlights surfaced:

The means to make it through. Yes, for sure, God's provision, the means.

Pumping gas at Bandera Road's Phillips station.

Hauling middle schoolers by yellow bus to and from their academic haunts.

An overly-generous and long-retired Kentucky schoolmarm.

My bread-and-butter news-print employer, the *San Antonio Express* towering opposite the *Alamo*.

Praying friends believing in a young couple's dream.

I also prized the instructors who pointed the way. I smiled at the medley of talent and personalities:

• Mister Irwin— health-food-eccentric whose relentless compassion often drew him off campus, to serve coffee and (ironically) sugary donuts to homesick soldiers and airmen. Men in uniform from the many bases encircling the city needed friends. Mr. Irwin readily pointed them toward the Best.

• Bob Lauver—the faculty's youngest and our energetic class sponsor.

• Ray Troyer—with the wisdom of a sage whose penetrating eyes seemed to mine my soul.

• Bill Hamon—dynamic, high-volume Pentateuch instructor whose prophetic bent later propelled him to a bigger platform.

• David Coote, Japanese-raised college president— his *Life of Christ* dramatizations marked by such a grasp of material and energetic flair students often laid aside their note-taking ball points to relish his imaginative scenes.

• Ruth Bell—sister to David, who as a little girl waded into Japan's icy river-waters to be baptized. A children's ministry power pack ever championing spiritual vision for the young. As with Ruth Bell Graham, this Ruth likewise bore a passion for the needy.

• John Hagee—master orator. When addressing a chapel service his keenly-honed sermons and powerful deliveries seized heart and mind of any preacher-wannabe in the room.

But among things I prized in my Bible school years, nothing matched the volumes of raw scripture text J. Andrew Freeborn encouraged us to ingest. Standing at his lectern, this serious academic packed in a 5 foot 9 inch frame, coaxed every student to Bible memorization. Unforgettable.

His *Romans* course found every student doggedly

rehearsing chapter eight and chapter twelve —sixty verses. For some, that figure seemed modest. But for students whose minds had only filed away a handful of passages, the challenge was great.

And then, when it came to the book of *Ephesians,* it was quite another issue.

"Alright ladies and gentlemen!"

Mister Freeborn lifted his voice against the shuffling of papers and classroom furniture as we settled in. "Today we move to Ephesians, a letter Paul penned while confined in a Roman prison cell.

"Now, Listen up, folks." His voice warmly serious. "I am here to make a pledge today, a promise to each of you taking this course." Pausing, he scanned the room, until every eye turned his way.

"Memorize all the book, and here is my pledge. You will be graded an 'A' for the course. That's right, you'll have your 'A', and that means regardless how you perform on exams or how your assignments may turn out.

"So, I challenge you. . . I welcome you. Commit to memory the whole book of Ephesians, reciting it to me at the end of semester, and get your perfect mark." He paused. "Agreed?"

Some heads nodded. Several students accepted the challenge, myself among them.

One hundred fifty-five verses, totaling three thousand twenty-two words. Although a few came close (over many late nights and gallons of black coffee), none of us hit the teacher's mark. Still, the exercise carried its own reward. Freeborn knew the exercise would enrich us, both personally and for ministry. Indeed, *Ephesians* captivated us — heart and soul — endearing itself to many from that very day.

With a letter from IBC's David Coote in hand, recommending us to pastors who might support our Africa vision, my LPN and I set out. Painfully conscious of my inexperience at fund-raising, I was both sobered and assured. Our trust must be in One wiser than ourselves.

Settling into the bucket seats of our freshly-loaded *Tempest*, we turned to each other. Excited. Nervous.

Our hands touched across the car's console and we prayed. I turned the key. "Here we go, Lord."

Chapter Nine

LIMA

MY EYEBROWS FURROWED as we crossed into Pennsylvania. We took in the expanse of her rolling hills, farmlands and forests. I was puzzled, *Where are the sky-scrapers?*

New York bewildered me even more. Any Oklahoman "knew" Yankee states were smothered under asphalt and concrete. As we motored northward from South Texas, our ever-expanding world called out my ignorance on the lay of the land. No wonder some northerners doubt whether Okies own cars.

Finally, I eased our auto to a halt. Before us stood an aged, four-story building perched atop a hill in a New York village. Lima. The month was January and a frigid drizzle descended, slow motion. The night was dark, and no one showed their presence. I turned to my wife, now in the early months of her first pregnancy.

"Seems we're here, darlin'. The sign out front says, *Elim.*"

Genesee Wesleyan Seminary, one of the first coed schools in the U.S., had opened its doors on this hill in 1831. Elim's training center now occupied several ornate structures of past times.

"Welcome, Jerry and Ann." Our cold reception, climate-wise, was countered by warm greetings of agency staff the next morning.

"Oklahoma, that's where you're from?" The office manager's eyes brightened. "You'll have to meet Ron and Jerry." Noting our blank look, he went on. "Ron Childs is from here in the Northeast. He and his wife, Jerry, have also come to us as missionary candidates. Jerry Childs is from down your way. Oklahoma."

Two days passed and we met the Childs, also bound for Africa. At her first greeting the cheery lady's voice betrayed her origin, the familiar drawl of my home state. I smiled inside.

Ann was quickly drawn to the small bundle Jerry cradled in her arms. "What a sweet little one you have there. . . a girl?"

The mother nodded. "Yes, Sarah. Like to hold her?"

My wife drew near, her own mama-instincts already roused.

Taking Sarah, she drew her close, little dreaming what lay ahead between the two in another time and place.

"Elim's meeting spot for worship is that big building just down there."

The Tabernacle, nestled along a hillside, its doors swung wide as students and faculty streamed in for chapel service. During the second musical piece, my thoughts drifted. I noticed a difference between this and other worship settings I had known. A difference with hymnbooks. My mind went back to Oklahoma, to my childhood place of worship.

"If a person had no access to the Bible through all his lifetime but owned the collection of Charles Wesley's Hymns, he would have

all that is needed for salvation's offer, the way of living fully in Christ and in the eternal hope of heaven." - Geoffrey Hawksley

The faded blue hymnals lay underneath the baby-grand up front, heaped in two stacks. Their pages were left unopened most of the year. Melodies resting muted inside the hard-bound covers like eager choir members, mouths duct-taped shut.

During my adolescent days I mused over the ritual of the song books. *I'm glad they're around, but why do they most of the time just sit there stacked up, nearly never touched?*

"Today, let's use the song books." The pastor's voice would ring, wistfully.

Thus on a random Sunday morning twice or so a year, out the faded books would come, a film of dust crowning the topmost volumes. A pair of youngsters would be called up, and the hymnals passed along church rows. Shortly the piano's intro to a tune, "In the Garden" followed by "Rock of Ages" or "I'll Fly Away." Finally, a piece or two penned by the beloved sightless composer, Fanny Crosby.

In those days of the 1950's I gazed at the stacks but could not understand their deep sentimental hold. The church's older members, whose voices rang out the lyrics with gusto, had become nearly weaned from the hymns of the church.

Music in the old blue books was deemed lacking the revivalist flavor preferred by a recent strain of Pentecostal-ism. Spiritual songs — lively choruses freshly-composed in the days of the *Latter Rain Movement* — replaced old hymn-books and vintage lyrics.

I grew fond of a musical heritage marked by informal choruses. Through their melodies, I found myself immersed in a worshipful presence, leading to rejoicing and deep-hearted release to praise. Times like those, often left worshippers reluctant to leave the sanctuary, well after the dismissal prayer.

Still, as years moved on, an undefined something in the realm of lyric and melody seemed missing. Like an absent-without-leave expression specially-tailored to hearts of God-seekers.

Reigning my thoughts back to the present *Tabernacle* setting, I sensed a pull, a homesick-kind of beckoning into rich melodies and lyrics of the past. *Maybe it was the little red book. Maybe my soul being highjacked by the Redemption hymnal.* Our next chapel service confirmed my suspicion.

"Good morning everyone. Let's stand, shall we? Please open to. . . ."

Responding to David Edwards' crisp Welsh tone, we reached for a nearby copy of *Redemption Songs*.

The collection of hymns spanned centuries, sung more widely by European than American worshippers. Some songs had been inspired in recent decades but many from long before, numbering near a thousand.

The Welshman continued with telling conviction, "We want to lay aside the morning's cares and those of the evening to come. The Lord is here, meeting with us. . . such a good, great and worthy Lord."

It was Edwards himself who had introduced *Redemption Songs* to Elim, and he encouraged us again. "His Spirit meets with us gathered now."

The parade of lyrics — inviting, warm, lofty in their message — drew us in.

From *O for a Thousand Tongues* to *O Worship the King,* to *Love Divine All Loves Excelling.* . . .

Penned by past-slave-trader to fine-art composer and others in between, the old melodies rallied anew. Humble artists proved themselves masters of prose. Of rhythms. Of holiness. Havergal, Spafford and Newton, Cowper, Scriven and Wesley. Like musical wine sellers, opening to us their vintage treasures. Inspiration for many hymns drawn from a composer's hardships. From sufferings. Limpings.

The assembly of young people gathered in the quaint New York village came alive in joyous praise. Leaving the hillside chapel an hour later, I felt an inner beckoning, an invitation to drink. From rich springs of ancient truth set to music. Through hymns. And found grace to respond to the welcome and not look back.

Chapter Ten

BUTTERFLIES

THE EXCITEMENT and angst Ann and I felt while passing into the conference room was palpable. How would we be received by Elim's Executive Missions Board? Would the elders usher us forward to the field? *Are we too young, too wet-behind-the-ears? What if they ask us to pastor in the states, first? We're not called as pastors. . . . Am I imagining it, or is my shirt collar sweat-soaked?*

Whatever angst we brought gradually eased. Discussion drew to a close and the Elim Council prayed, commissioning us with blessing.

◊◊◊

Unblinking, my wife took the medical release document and tucked it inside her passport. Stamped *Canandaigua, N.Y.,* her doctor's letter okayed her transatlantic flight. We would board for Kenya May 26, just forty-nine days ahead of our first baby's *Africa* due date. But first to Brooklyn in the Big Apple.

Having packed and shipped off three 55-gallon steel drums of earthly possessions, we were eastward-bound to Brooklyn. We would lodge overnight at an inner-city mission in a sketchy area. Next day we would head to JFK Airport and board an outbound flight.

"Where have you been?" We detected the edge in the director's voice.

The Inner-City Mission he led bordered a crowded collection of gray multi-storied dwellings. The neighborhood pulsed with evidence of addiction and vice. We should have known better.

"We took a stroll around the block. Maybe a couple blocks."

"Please. . . ," The director's eyes pleaded. "Never do that kind of thing in this area — not without one of our staff."

We meekly nodded compliance.

Next day an extrovert driver at the Mission eagerly chimed, "Hey guys, before I take you to the airport, let's swing through Coney Island." Assisting my great-with-child wife into the old van, I helped her settle onto a bench seat. Of things we had looked forward to on our first NYC visit, dodging Coney Island's pot holes at head-clunking speed had not made the list.

"I wonder what that was all about?" Ann whispered a moan on the jostling return to our lodging, patting her extended midsection. "What was the attraction?", she went on, "Seems he hoped to rush the arrival of our little bundle." Next day, our luggage secure, we boarded the Brooklyn Mission van a final time, and waved the staff goodbye.

Nine years after *Idlewild* took the name JFK International Airport we shuffled our way into the belly of America's most-celebrated passenger aircraft. The cavernous Boeing 747, aptly nicknamed *Jumbo Jet*.

Seat-belts fastened, we took each other's hands and whispered a prayer. The moment felt surreal. Here we were, en route to the great continent we had so longed to reach — to serve for years to come.

The leg to England was relaxed, given the adrenaline-charged hours leading up to it. We needed relaxation, considering what lay ahead. The surprise news from Elim's office two days earlier was fresh.

"Jerry and Ann, we've just learned of a change. You'll arrive in England at London's Heathrow but will fly out from Gatwick, several miles away by bus."

Changing planes in London we had expected. Changing airports, we had not.

Heathrow. The world's busiest airport.

I gathered up assorted luggage along with typewriter and guitar. Piling them into the small London bus, I helped my waddling wife aboard. Ann rested her head against my shoulder.

An hour later, I spotted the Gatwick sign. "We're here, Hon."

"Okay. Be sure to bring all the pieces. . . don't forget the typewriter."

As I helped Ann down and reached for our baggage, we agreed the hour ride had been pleasant. We rolled through quaint country-side past communities with uncommon names: Egham, Chertsey, Weybridge.

What fanciful names will we find in Kenya? Plenty, no doubt.

For now, we knew of Nairobi — a place we soon would call another name.

Home.

But not yet.

"Sir? Madame? May I see your passports?"

Handing them over to the agent, this was our first hint at anything amiss.

"We need to keep these for a bit," he said, clutching our precious eagle-embossed documents. "We are checking some irregularities."

Irregularities?

Chapter Eleven

EMBAKASI

"THE TRAVEL COMPANY your organization elected to use has possibly violated air travel rulings. We've been cooperating in a precautionary investigation."

"Oh. . . hmm. . . when, sir may we have our documents returned?" I found myself wanting to mimic the British accent with its more officious tone. His response came crisp but courteous. "We shall be back with you shortly." I interrupted.

"Sir, I'm wondering. With the twelve-hour layover underway, my wife here could use a quiet spot somewhere to rest. Is there. . ."

He turned to Ann. "Oh, Indeed, madam!" An attendant was beckoned.

The agent moved around a counter and out of sight, our passports in hand. Thus far, I had suppressed my anxiety. Now it bumped up a degree.

The documents got back to us, approved and duly stamped. I was happy to find Ann resting on a small bed in a comfy airport side room.

"Ladies and gentlemen, passengers will now begin boarding British Caledonia's flight to Nairobi.

◊◊◊

Southward past Western Europe, across the Mediterranean and over the Sahara, our big aircraft made its way to the land of our calling. The plane set down in Kenya just after sunrise. It seemed fitting, as we would now enter the dawn of a new chapter in our lives. One of vision, of mystery. One of fruitfulness, we hoped. Here, in this new land.

Africa.

◊◊◊

"Jerry Lout, right?"

The New Zealand accent came from beyond a railing at the immigration line. John Maxwell reached beyond a barrier and pushed an official-looking paper my direction. With our carry-ons, we shuffled our way toward a small, windowed booth in which sat an immigration officer. The spot where a visas may be either green-lighted, rejected or held for review.

The paper handed me was my work permit, a critically-needed item for our long-term stay. The permit's signature scrawled beneath a richly-inked stamp, assured our passage to the luggage zone.

Mile-high Embakasi Airport sat a short distance beyond Nairobi Game Park, popular tourist attraction at the city's edge. The Maasai word, Nairobi, meaning "cool water" had anchored itself firmly on the Kenya map. Six more years would pass before Embakasi's rechristening — its new name paying homage to the country's first president: *Jomo Kenyatta International Airport.*

John's wife, Jenny, announced cheerily, "Seems your luggage all made it fine." Her two pre-school boys stirred at our feet. Noting Ann's larger-than-life condition, one asked, "Mummy, will Auntie have her baby now?"

Though wearied from travel, Ann was lifted by the young mother's warm suggestion, "Let's get you where you can relax a bit, shall we?" Jenny was Nairobi born-and-raised, as comfortably at home in Africa as any *expatriate*. From the outset our households bonded.

Another woman, her hair graying about the temples, chimed a hearty, "Welcome, Kiddos!" The American accent stirred a good feeling.

Eva Butler fit the role of a matronly, plucky veteran of Africa's bush-country. Single-mom of two and mission's servant to several remote tribes.

In her company, Ann and I felt a measure of awe. Once I made the connection of Eva's family roots, a warm chuckle rose inside me. I took a moment to savor again the cheery greeting given not long ago in a Texas school chapel, "So this is the man with the black heart." Eva Butler, Carlton Spencer's sister. We would learn of a difficult and finally dissolved marriage, of a single mother of two – a son and daughter – venturing into the demanding life of missionary service in equatorial Africa.

In a few days I would visit a nomadic region Eva called home. And get a taste of raw fear.

◊◊◊

I had never known a housing edition named by alphabet. A short hop from the airport the station wagon eased up to Maxwell's *South C* home.

The house sat hidden behind a stonework wall, like a shy

maiden partly-concealed behind a fortress of vines. Bougainvillea with their rich array of petals. Pinks, purples, oranges and reds garnishing much of the 'C' neighborhood.

Back in San Antonio, Raymond Troyer blessed me with my first-ever 35mm camera. *What beauty, these African flowers. To capture their images by a finger click. If I can just remember Ray's tips on how to use the thing.*

Our landing in Kenya came early Sunday.

Jenny Maxwell sang out, "We're off to morning church. You folks just relax. . . sleep a bit if you can. . . you've travelled far and long. After service we'll come collect you and go for lunch. Okay?"

Weariness had overtaken us, and we happily agreed. After all, Sunday was a day of rest.

Our first meal in Africa? What would it be? And where? As green travelers, we imagined dining in a mud hut under a grass roof. Until we passed through Nairobi Hilton's entryway. *Ah. The country's biggest revenue came through tourism — her wild game parks and all.*

An hour later, we left the hotel's café, happily filled with sandwiches and fries. *Chips,* I coached myself. *Fries are not 'fries' here. They're chips.*

On our first day in Africa, a living tutorial greeted us, with a host of lessons ahead. Kenya was a land rich in contrasts, impoverished and wealthy, tradition-steeped yet cutting-edge, separated (40+ tribes) and united.

We had barely begun to learn. It sobered and inspired us that we could start now. Here at tourism's iconic Hilton – walking-distance from one of the continent's largest slums – Mathare Valley.

"Eva needs electrical wiring done at her *Mashuru* place," offered my host. "The job should take a couple days. Like to come?"

"Sure, John." Getting away from the big city and out to real Africa seemed fun, even a thrill. Walking alone and unarmed through wild game country had not crossed my mind.

Jim Reeves? I could detect the country swooner's velvet voice anywhere. But Africa's bush country?

Chapter Twelve

THAT SINKING FEELING

STRAINS of the ballad floated my direction from a battery-powered cassette player beyond a giant anthill. *What sheer power music has, to carry a guy back in time.* I imagined an Oklahoma hay-field. A sandwich break on a humid day.

John and I had come to a remote Maasai village, a map's dot north of the Tanzania border.

"Wow. What a scene!" The snowy summit of legendary Mount Kilimanjaro peeked from behind billowy clouds, her beauty hypnotic.

"Ready to hunt some wild game?"

John and I had finished a wiring job on Eva's cottage. Time for a little adventure. As for hunting arsenal, his 35mm Canon would do.

The VW Beetle cast a late afternoon shadow. John eased the car to a spot overlooking a murky brown pool. *Nice watering hole for some exotic beast.* The region was big game hunting territory for all manner of wildlife. *Would an elephant or a rhino show? A lion, maybe. . . leopard?*

After a fruitless half-hour waiting, John touched the ignition.

"Here's an idea," John said, a mix of daring and mischief flavoring his voice. "During these months, the river stays mainly dry. Its path winds along a few kilometers and eventually passes near Eva's place. What say we take the bug right up the river instead of going back along the *murram* road?" Though he hadn't yet been a year in Kenya, John was the missionary veteran.

"Sure. Why not?"

Africa's equatorial sun lowered to the horizon, the night hastily spreading darkness along the riverbed. Dense forest hemmed us at either side. And two young men pondered how to free a Volkswagen Beetle sunk axle-deep in river-bottom sand.

The idea we'd hatched seemed sensible at the time. My new friend had steered the Bug downward, into the wide river bed. "Here we go. Should reach Eva's place in a jif!"

A few minutes steady movement up the center of the river, then, "Hey John, why the sudden drag?"

He was quiet as the car's tires lost traction with each sluggish advance. The sand's texture here had changed. The finer granules seemed hungry to gulp up Volkswagen tires. Spinning, spinning. The car dug in. Forward movement ceased. We were stuck.

Ditching the plan to make it back to Eva's via the riverbed, we'd try turning the car around. The daunting task then, to escape this oversized sand-pit we'd landed ourselves in.

"Jerry, here's an idea."

I had heard that phrase before.

Chapter Thirteen

NIGHT SWEATS

MY FRIEND'S newest scheme made nervous sense. "Whoever is at the wheel, the other pushes from behind. The driver must *not* slow the vehicle, no matter what."

Simple enough. The guy behind the car, the one pushing, will likely hoof his way out, reuniting with car and driver in due time. We would leave the dried-up tributary behind, all happening in the dead of night. We simply *had* to get the VW out and back to the dusty road.

My turn to push.

"Come on, little bug", I coaxed, energy draining out my boot soles.

John's foot to the accelerator, the vehicle picked up speed.

"Good," I panted, "keep going, keep going." Traction took hold and my Kiwi partner shifted to second gear. The bug was on its way. My reserves spent, I could not marshal enough strength to leap aboard the rear bumper. *Foolish notion, anyway.*

Shoulders drooping, I waved John on. The car gained speed. As the distance between us grew, I rehearsed our pledge. *Keep the car in motion.* The bug must not slow and risk her tires spinning again.

I recalled something else. This was Africa's wild where the term "ferocious" implied a broad range of animal kin.

My panting slowed as I squinted at the dusky landscape. Sketchy outlines of treetops marked distant river banks. All else between the trees and myself was utterly dark. A night cry from some undefined animal sounded.

I watched the car grow smaller, the space between us widen. Nothing captured the isolation I felt when the VW passed out of view. Its dwarfed taillights vanished around a bend. The motoring sound faded, softened further, then went silent. The dark about me seemed tangible, so much I could feel it. My body tightened.

I had never been more afraid.

Passing on foot through wildlife terrain is not advised, especially when unarmed. Alone. After dark.

Try as I may, I could not shut my mind to a growing parade of frightful images: *a Cape Buffalo lifting its great head, sniffing the night air, catching my scent. . . a deadly viper lying unseen on the darkened sand before me. . . a Leopard. Strong. Ferocious.*

A chill passed through me as I imagined her, mid-flight— a great leap — her claws and teeth bared.

My heart-beats outpaced my footsteps. *This panic must stop. Get control, man. Do something.*

Call up Scripture.

The thought came strong yet calm — a *voice* from within fostered a quiet tone. Pressing my mind to respond, I willed it past taunting images. Mentally scrolled phrases that lay present in memory stores. I paused at the great hymn book of the Bible—the Psalms.

To *Psalm 91,* a favorite. And timely for the moment. I

needed this psalm. Even more, I needed particular statements found there. Crisp. Bold. Assuring. By a miracle, I found my voice. Keeping my brisk pace, I breathed the phrases toward the unlit sky.

He that dwelleth in the secret place of the Most High shall abide under the shadow of the Almighty.

I will say of the Lord, he is my refuge and my fortress: my God; in him will I trust.

Surely, he shall deliver thee from the snare of the fowler, and from the noisome pestilence.

He shall cover thee with his feathers, and under his wings shalt thou trust: his truth shall be thy shield and buckler. . . Thou shalt not be afraid for the terror by night; nor for the arrow that flieth by day. . . .

I continued quoting. Gained courage as though a strong old conviction half-asleep were suddenly stirred awake. Even my heartbeat seemed to thump a more natural rhythm.

A thousand shall fall at thy side, and ten thousand at thy right hand; but it shall not come nigh thee.

Thou hast made the Lord, which is my refuge, even the Most High, thy habitation;

There shall no evil befall thee, neither shall any plague come nigh thy dwelling.

For he shall give his angels charge over thee, to keep thee in all thy ways.

They shall bear thee up in their hands, lest thou dash thy foot against a stone.

By now, a richer boldness visited. Peace, a near-tangible sense of well-being, enclosed me. A final phrase surfaced. It clinched the matter.

Thou shalt tread upon the lion and adder: the young lion and the dragon shalt thou trample under feet.

Wonderfully free of fear. I smiled, realizing my hasty

march had slowed. *No, Lord, it doesn't seem you brought me to Africa that I become food for the big cats or victim to the cobra's fang. Thank you.*

As I resumed a clipped stride, moments sped by. I navigated the river's long bend and spied the familiar image. There she sat, the beloved little Beetle.

Because he hath set his love upon me. . . He shall call upon me, and I will answer him: I will be with him in trouble; I will deliver him and honor him.

The bug sat well out of the riverbed, its high beams revealing the murram track ahead. A few steps and I was there. Nervous laughter from both of us.

"Let's get on over to Eva's place. She might be worried."

Chapter Fourteen

TIMELY MERRIMENT

LANGUAGE CLASSES STARTED and not a day too soon. I was ready for routine. One day I went to check the mail.

The key slipped easily into its slot. I was downtown Nairobi, standing before a bank of metal post office boxes. Ours proclaimed its rank in bold digits, 30207. Drawing out the few pieces of mail bearing our name, I paused, noting one with an Alabama postmark. I knew the sender though we hadn't been in touch since my San Antonio departure over a year ago. I turned the envelope a couple of times. *How about that. . . what's Ray up to these days?*

Ann and I had passed through our first Kenya months in a blur, a lot of *new* happenings. New friends, new apartment, new culture and car. . . New *baby.*

Julie Ann Lout made her squalling entry in Nairobi Hospital July 13, 1972 —a bare six weeks after our Africa landing. The most joyous moment for us since Ann and I had pledged to each other our vows.

Then, a few weeks in, I engaged another kind of new. New language.

Our funds were short —not enough contributions to cover an insurance payment due *and* my Swahili School entrance fee. By now the studies were underway, but the money worries weighed on me.

Hours before my post office visit, I had wakened in the pre-dawn hours. Our studio flat came with an oddly arranged self-contained kitchen, making possible an inviting space for alone-time. Before boiling water for coffee, I knelt and soon found myself questioning.

Laugh? I'm to laugh?

The question was my response to an unexpected but strong impression I felt moments after kneeling, *"Laugh. . . give your voice to laughing. . . simply laugh."* To consult with my feelings over it seemed pointless. What I *felt* to do was any number of things. Return to bed. Bemoan our money shortfall. Worry.

The word "laugh" persisted, like a clear nudge.

Okay, here goes.

"Hahaha. . . hahaha. . . hahaha."

The sounds slipping quietly off my tongue were flat, lifeless as a corpse, seeming to ricochet off the wall's bright yellow paint. My face offered no expression signaling pleasure. *Alright. I'll smile.*

I willed my face to the posture and soon sensed the Lord's Spirit stir me.

The period of hollow chuckling offered upward stretched into a minute and more. For the most part my eyes remained open, the practice not seeming quite like prayer.

What happened next took me by surprise. A gradual surprise if that's possible.

The joy-stream inside me began as a trickle and broadened soon to a rippling brook, before bursting out in overflow. In moments the stream surged upward like Old Faithful awash in laughter.

The contrast astonished me. My earlier mood, weary and disheartened, suddenly displaced by free-spirited rejoicing. After a time, I sat restful on the floor's cool surface. Quiet. At peace.

Irrational, even hypocritical as the laughing exercise first seemed, my lame ha-ha-ha's had at some juncture bridged a threshold. Persistence fostered the passing of a baton to an unencumbered spirit of laughter.

Regardless the mystery, I was certain a shift had happened.

The money-worry lifted, vanished. Still I was rational, knowing a full day of normal, responsible activities lay ahead.

Four hours later at the post office I spotted the envelope marked Birmingham. I peeled it open.

"Hi Jerry and Ann. I hope you all are doin' well."

I smiled, recalling Ray Manguno's gentle Cajun brogue.

"I'm out in Alabama's back-country holding evangelistic meetings. Preaching some night services at a little church. . . ."

Ray spoke of a practice he'd taken up when holding week-long revival meetings.

"I always preach one night of the week on foreign missions, and afterward I raise an offering. We pass the plate so the folks can send a gift to whoever the church supports."

As I read, curiosity stirred. A folded insert dropped from the envelope.

Ray continued, "When the service ended the pastor came over to me a little embarrassed. He said, 'Brother Raymond, our church doesn't support any missionary. In fact, we don't even *know* a missionary. . . Do you know anybody that could use tonight's offering?'"

"'Well, pastor, I actually have a couple on my mind right now.'"

"Now, Brother Jerry and Ann, I want to say this. In the past few days you've been in my thoughts. In fact, images of you all came to my mind ahead of me preaching here at this church on missions.

"So anyway, that kind of explains how the enclosed gift is for you. I hope it's a blessing."

Taking the few steps to our white VW marked by its KNZ 948 license plate, I silently rehearsed the story, slowly re-reading Raymond's letter, word by word. Taking in the dollar amount registered on the check I knew would precisely cover our outstanding bills.

The car windows closed, I let out a whoop. "Praise you, praise you Father! Thank you, thank you, Lord!"

Wait 'til Ann sees this. Steering the Volkswagen into traffic, I added extra foot-weight to the accelerator.

Chapter Fifteen

ABSENT WITHOUT LEAVE

THANKSGIVING. . . *What? Tomorrow?*

My eyes squinting, I stared at the square box marked Thursday in the American-designed date ledger. And blurted the discovery. "Ann, take a look at this calendar. Tomorrow's *Thanksgiving!*"

"Really? You sure?"

For two months Swahili studies had taken most of my time. Noun classes, prefixes, infixes, suffixes, vocabulary. . . . My Okie tongue wrestled non-stop trying to mimic Bantu sounds.

Language class this Wednesday had wrapped up like any other. Leaving the school's Anglican-sponsored compound, I headed home to our flat and spotted the calendar lying open to the current month. November. It mocked me.

The surprise arrival of Thanksgiving Eve stirred emotion. I felt a bit indignant that such a sacred holiday should count as just another pair of digits on a calendar leaf. Irrational feeling this, for one living in another country, but present all the same.

Thanksgiving's tomorrow. But so are Swahili classes.

The contest inside me was brief.

"Honey, I'm cutting classes tomorrow. How about a picnic?"

Thanksgiving morning of 1972 arrived gorgeous. Just months earlier Kentucky Fried Chicken had launched their finger-lickin' enterprise in Nairobi. What image better reflects American tradition than Colonel Sanders?

Ann bundled our four-month-old in a colorful blanket. The aroma of KFC filled our Volkswagen as we moved toward City Park.

A generous splash of jacaranda and bougainvillea – purples, greens, reds – surrounded us under sunny skies. A light breeze stirred as I laid out the blanket. Ann held our little one close as she found a resting spot.

We sat cross-legged and reviewed a few "Turkey days" of our past. Memories stirred gratitude. Our four months now in this land still seemed surreal.

Infant Julie gurgled. I scanned the garden environment and voiced a thanks to him who put it all together. For bringing us to this beautiful, hurting land. For one another here, out under the open sky. For family back home.

Turning to Ann, it was time I voiced a request with proper grammatical care, applying the polite form, *"Naomba kuku, tafadhali?"* (Some chicken please?)

We laughed at my language exercise for the day. It would have to do.

◊◊◊

"Jerry, meet Charles Duke. He's been to the moon." Hardly an introduction one met with every day. The gentleman smiled. "Charlie," he said.

I took the extended hand. "Pleased to meet you, sir. I'm Jerry."

Only ten pairs of astronaut boots had left their print on the lunar surface and, of those space men, he was the youngest.

Shaking the Colonel's hand added a link to my feeling connected, however remotely, to the daring venture NASA had successfully undertaken. Later I would ponder, *How many Apollo blueprints, with their complex equations and images, had I sorted and filed at the Tulsa plant with their engineerish terms, Reaction Control Thruster Assembly and the like?*

Charles Duke was now in Africa to deliver to the National Museum a Kenya flag that made it to the moon and back.

Duke had set foot on the moon a month before my wife and I landed on Kenya soil. I joined a gathering that evening where the astronaut recounted his moon walk and his story of personal faith. The room grew quiet as his talk shifted away from topics of science and space travel.

The astronaut's final statement of the evening moved the listeners. Like an enduring bootprint on the lunar surface, it left an impression for a long time.

"Travelling to outer space was indeed amazing. Yet I've discovered since, that walking on the moon does not compare with walking on the earth with the Son."

Chapter Sixteen

DRUMBEATS IN THE DARK

"HEY GARY, got a minute? It's my water pump. . . got a clatter goin' on."

Minutes later, socket and ratchet in hand, the wiry young man wriggled beneath the fellow student's clunker, feeling as much at home here as an armadillo in the August heat of Texas. Gary Pokorney's later achievement in a Far East land left his friends mildly amazed.

Gary was no slouch, as his dogged probing of carburetors and gear boxes testified. The college parking lot supplied an endless number of projects.

A couple years flew past. My wife and I settled into life on the great African continent. Checking for mail one day, I drew from the PO box a fresh copy of my alma mater's paper. Traveling surface mail over land and across ocean, seven weeks coming.

A lead article in Hallelujah Hill's *Torchbearer*: "Gary Pokorney honored for Oratory Feat."

Phrases leapt from the newsprint, ". . . Pokorney wins first place. . . nationwide oratorical contest. . . Korea's First Lady hosts reception. . . ."

I completed the piece and shook my head, amazed and happy for my friend. Over dinner, Ann and I recalled scenes from our lives on the *Hill*, special friendships, memories.

I glanced her way. "To think, babe, First Place. The wife of the nation's head of state hosted a special tea in Gary's honor. And the president of the country himself even said he would have sworn – judging by Gary's voice – that he was a Korean national."

Moving to our small desk, I sat before our little Hermes typewriter.

"Dear Gary, we just got news of your achievement. Wow! Congratulations!" My post script followed, "I do want you to know this. When I discovered your achievement, I retreated to my room. Seating myself in sackcloth and ashes, I wept over my Swahili-English dictionary."

Language school wrapped up and we joined with friends to celebrate Christmas. The new year came, and we loaded up the VW. Journeyed west, toward our new home.

◊◊◊

"Do you hear something, Hon?"

The drum sounds reached our ears, distant and eerie, more dreamlike than real. Indeed, I thought at first the rhythmic thumping *was* a dream. But as the drumming — joined now by human voices — grew in volume, our feelings of unease heightened. As young missionaries freshly assigned to our new posting, we lay still, wide-eyed in our pitch-dark bedroom within this remote mission house. Our breathing shallowed.

"They're coming closer."

Taranganya occupied a tiny dot on the rare Kenya map that would count the outpost worthy of any mention at all. The village's calling card included a butcher shop. Flies gathered to hike over slabs of beef suspended on iron hooks well before the time customers savored the meat. We learned how the pressure cooker claimed a prized spot in the home of any self-respecting missionary.

Along the bend in the village road, two schools' book-ended the butchery, one for elementary kids, the other serving high-schoolers. Our mission station home lay steps away from the butcher shop.

The station rested on the uppermost slope of a gradually-ascending hill. Its entrance-point marked the head of a sweeping curve of the narrow, unpaved road passing in front. Our new lodging lay in a remote sector of Kenya just five miles north of Tanzania's unpatrolled border. The glistening waters of Lake Victoria rested 40 miles to our west.

We newbie missionaries, with little orientation about our new setting, had just moved hundreds of miles to Bukuria Mission. We had no history with any person of the Kuria Tribe.

The drumming and the voices drew nearer. Chanting sounds in a local dialect unknown to us increased the angst.

Had we pondered more the impact of faith since the gospel's arrival a couple decades earlier, our jittery nerves would have stirred less.

The night of fitful sleep finally passed. Next morning, we asked the obvious question as the midnight drum-beats and chanting voices called up old film images of painted warriors, pith helmets and boiling pots.

Embarrassed chuckles came once we traced our Saturday night insomnia to a small band of *Kuria* believers on their way to a prayer meeting.

◊◊◊

Bukuria. Our first upcountry home.

Bukuria — where a tornado uprooted trees and ripped the metal roof from our neighbor's house. The twister hurled it across the compound, pretzelling corrugated sheets high in branches on its way out.

Bukuria — the kind of place that stirs nostalgia. Past residents savored old images of hazy smoke clouds wafting over distant Maasai plains. Evidence of herdsmen purging brown grasslands before the onset of March rains.

A watchman, Nyamahanga, became a fixed night-time presence at the station, greeting us on our arrival. His armor consisted of a homemade bow with a handful of arrows (razor sharp). We had heard of tribal skirmishes flaring up in the region now and then. One wouldn't want to be caught in the cross-fire, or worse, as the actual target of an agitated tribesman.

Lord, thanks for watching over us, over this place. Help us to add something of good by being here.

Chapter Seventeen

BUMPY LANDING

JERRY LOUT, seasoned missionary. Not.

Green – Naïve – Novice - Ignorant. String them together you had my name tag.

The rambling house my wife, myself and our bundle of Julie settled into had been built by pioneering missionaries, years before our coming. The pioneers had fashioned the dwelling from local soil, rust-tinted bricks fired in a home-built kiln.

A day or two after our Bukuria arrival, a chorus of male voices took us by surprise. Not a musical chorus but a mix of busy voices growing loud, fading a little, then loud again.

Are they angry. . . enthused. . . something other. . .which?

Their language was neither English nor Swahili. *Kikuria, no doubt.* Unsure of their disposition and ignorant of who they were, I touched the screen door. Then moved to the open veranda where the dozen or so Africans stood assembled.

I was twenty-seven, my wife twenty-three. It was clear most of the men, while not elderly, out-seasoned me — their skin weathered from years under a tropical sun.

The group of strangers arriving unannounced, left me uneasy.

Do we invite them in? If so, what next? Are these gents all friendly to the Mission. . . We have a six-month-old girl.

We were out of our element, in waters we had not swum.

One of the older men – *their spokesman?* – moved closer. His English was broken, his accent challenging but I could make it out easily enough.

"We come to greet. We come to welcome you here to this place."

I drew near.

"Hello", nodding. "Hello", smiling. "Hello", I greeted, shaking each extended hand one by one. Though I did feel more at ease and was touched by their welcoming us to Kuria-land, I still wasn't confident how to respond. Only to offer repeatedly. "Thank you, Thank you, sir. Thank you.

I searched awkwardly for some cultural bridge to temper the situation. Answers eluded me. The visitors glanced toward one another, voiced some quiet, mysterious words. And eventually, slowly, went their way.

It was months before I learned I had made a marked impression that unsettling day. It took a while to redeem our name — the word on the street, "They did not even welcome us in for tea."

So there it was. The new resident-missionary come to live and serve among the *Wakuria* people successfully offended a welcoming delegation of church elders.

Like the snaking roadway leading past the Mission, further bends in the road lay surely ahead — our Taranganya learning curve.

Most people the world over forgive offenses done by newcomers — especially when the error is made in ignorance.

We found the statement true, at least among the Kuria. Our failure as green missionaries to extend basic "please-enter-for-a-cup-of-tea" hospitality, drew no further mention from the poorly-treated delegation.

◊◊◊

"Hello, I am Reverend Joseph Muhingira."

I drew some comfort when Ann and I received a gracious welcome from the local Overseer.

Muhingira received us into his cement-plastered, tin-roofed home where his wife, Esther greeted us warmly. Entering the grounds, we noted several range cows brought in from their day of grazing. They jostled, mooing in the tight outdoor corral just beyond the dining room.

The holding pen was framed of rough-hewn poles fashioned from skinny, felled trees. Such timber dotted the rolling terrain of the region. Esther and her firstborn daughter served us our first Kuria meal: roast chicken, a local spinach-like green called Sukumawiki, a cup of broth served in a modest tin bowl. And Ugali.

Ugali, a kind of corn-meal mush, was brought to the table hot — baked firm, molded in a half-moon-shaped bowl. Esther deftly inverted the bowl, planting it top-down on a large plate. She lifted the metal bowl, leaving the spherical hill of odorless ugali steaming before us. We did catch the fragrance of a kerosene flame. It shone from the single lantern perched atop a seasoned chest-of-drawers at the edge of the tight dining area.

A staticky short-wave radio, powered by D-size batteries, rested on the same furniture piece. From it rang a distinct mix of African tones, high-pitched, electric guitar-plinking blended with smooth Swahili vocalists. Passing "hole-in-the-wall" cafes months before along Nairobi's streets, I had wondered if more than just one song had found its way from a composer's pen. Since then I had made peace with the style's apparent monotony.

The lantern's glow thrust eerie shadows jittering and waltzing in irregular moves along a wall, a reflection of mother and daughter as they tended to the servings. We ate our fill and washed the remnants down with hot chai – cooked with sugar and milk thrown in together.

"*Mungu awabariki.*" Our first dining experience in Kuria-land ended as pleasantly as it began. Thanking our hosts with the Swahili "God bless you all," we stepped from the humble dwelling.

Overseer Muhingira led us on the foot-path to our little VW. A pleasant glow from the vivid Kenya moon played on Julie's upturned eyes and across the soft blanket couching her face. It gave the blanket a magical look.

The evening had gone well. Muhingira, gracious, gentleman-like and Esther's warm personality complimented her talents in the kitchen.

I turned the engine and we followed the dirt track home to the mission. In the quiet calm of the African night, it seemed we had moved to a peaceful wonderland.

Meeting our neighbor, Grace, and learning her story would challenge such thinking to the core.

Chapter Eighteen

SURPRISE CHRISTENING

"Excuse me, I need to what?"

"No, you need to help him along. You must show him the door. It's what you do here."

Moving from Bukuria to Suna brought new discoveries, new challenges. Many differences between these two tribes, the Kuria and Luo. Traditions. Customs. Worldview.

"Rally the courage, Jerry. . . and just do it."

Our colleagues, the Harmans, were off to Canada for a time. In their absence, it fell to Ann and me to oversee Suna Mission Station. Like Bukuria, Suna sat a stone's throw from Tanzania, 45 kilometers east of Lake Victoria.

My disquiet was brought on by a visit to our home by a nearby pastor to discuss church matters. Nothing weighty. A simple stop-in visit of informal business common to mission work.

By the time our second, then third visits rolled around over the coming days, I felt conflicted. Five words summed up my dilemma: *How do you part ways?* I was stumped over this cultural challenge. When does a visitor simply leave for home once a visit is done?

I had noted a pattern. . . .

————

"Welcome, Brother Thomas. Come on in." We would make our way to sitting-room chairs. Ann appeared, greeted the visitor, then moved toward the kitchen. Soon a kettle whistled. Cups of hot *chai* rested on a serving tray. So far so good.

The pastor then brought up a matter. In due course, I might introduce another. By now chai cup number two arrived and was drained. *Nothing odd here. . . the locals enjoyed their tea.*

By the time our third spicy-sweet chai was downed, our discussion matters had typically wrapped up. The pastor's visit was finished.

Thomas did not move. Nor did I.

The pastor checked his watch more than once, while I hoped my glances toward the wall clock weren't obvious. Creative snatches of small talk came and went, broken by a lingered moment of awkward silence.

Finally, in a series of courteous but uneasy back-and-forths, my visitor arose. I did the same, and Pastor Thomas was out the door. At last.

"Here's the thing, Jerry," my culture-savvy friend offered on hearing my dilemma.

"Once you're done with business or whatever, the visit is over. It's finished and it's time."

"Time for what?"

"Time to tell him to go home."

My eyebrows crinkled. "Say that again."

"Sure, it's like this. In this culture, see, it's really rude of a visitor to get up and — like westerners — just head for the door. We're used to the, Gotta'go now, see ya later' line. No, it's not like that here. Where you're living now, you must *invite* your guest to leave."

Hmm.

Before very long a chance to dismiss a house guest came my way. Pastor Thomas, again.

Twenty minutes into our chat about business at hand – with the second round of our tea cups riding on empty – we each knew a natural time had come to wrap up.

Though I had it on good counsel that my next move was a routine practice within the culture, still it would be my first time to actually tell a visitor to leave my house.

Inhaling a slow breath, I rose from my chair. Smiling broadly, I moved a couple steps his direction, extending my hand as though I felt comfortable. "Pastor Thomas, it's been good seeing you today. I'm glad you came by."

Before the phrase had fully left my lips, I caught a look in his eyes signaling there was a God in heaven. All was well in the world. Sending my visitor to the door was *not* an act of rudeness, rejection or stupidity.

The ready smile Thomas flashed conveyed warmth and pleasure — and likely, I thought to myself — a measure of relief. I felt in the moment I might be reading his thoughts, *Ah, my dear young American friend finally gets it!*

While taking up residence among a people not your own brings with it mystery and a cultural hurdle or two, we were finding that once sincere attempts were made to adapt, entry-ways to delightful surprises flung open.

◊◊◊

"Pastor Jerry, please may we welcome you and Sister Ann. Our new child has come! Meet us at our home for tea."

Ten months earlier the South Nyanza woman had stepped forward for prayer in our little Migori church. She and her husband wanted to grow a family but were unable to conceive. Her eyes pleaded, "Please pray."

We bowed. Sincere petition heavenward. Time moved on, months passed, and I had all but forgotten the morning's interchange.

Happily accepting the couple's invitation, we entered the simple home on a mid-afternoon. Brand new parents, overtaken with joy, shuttled folding chairs to the modest outdoor courtyard. We had been invited to celebrate with them the recent arrival of their newborn.

With our near-giddy hosts, we drank sweet *chai* and helped ourselves to servings of toasty, deep-fried *mandazis* (pastries).

An auntie appeared now from indoors, a blanketed infant nestled in her arms, the host's "miracle baby", a boy.

At such occasions a tribute of honor is often assigned a person deemed in some way helpful along the journey.

Surnames among the Luo people often begin with the letter 'O'.

"Thank you, Pastor Jerry, for praying with us back on that day." The mother paused, both she and her husband beaming,

"Now, meet *Jerry Lout Okech!*"

On any marathon journey of a missionary, special moments make time stand still, moments joyous, sacred, like no other. We drove away singing.

Chapter Nineteen

DISRUPTIVE VISIT

AFTER SOME WEEKS in our new location I found myself in a quandary rehearsing my earlier language-student days in Nairobi.

"La!"

The round, bald – at times gruff – language tutor prided himself in his home area's version of the Swahili language. After all, his was from the *Coast*. Only Kenya's neighbor to the south, Tanzania, could compete with the gold standard Swahili spoken along this man's Indian Ocean region. His voice was raspy, making him seem harsher than the students knew him to be. His sudden *"La!"* (*No!*) was instantly followed by a terse scold, *"Up-country* Swahili!" With little patience for poorly spoken words, the aging gent spat out the phrase as if evicting a live wasp from his mouth.

It was by this *mwalimu mzee* (elder instructor) I first caught the need to communicate well in another culture. The reality was further driven home once our stay in the Capital City ended. Through a much-loved missionary headmistress whose wrinkle-teased eyes constantly twinkled and whose tongue offered up wisdom and wit by the kilo. On the topic of foggy communication Elizabeth Ridenour liked serving up her tongue-in-cheek phrase, "I believe I understand what you think I said, but I'm not sure that what I said is what you thought I meant."

Some locations aren't best suited for a native English-speaker to learn the Swahili language. Nairobi was such a place. A recommended, though challenging way, to master a new language is through a method called *immersion learning.* Learning by immersion happens when everybody around the student understands and speaks the desired language, but everybody does *not* speak the *student's* language. A sink or swim approach.

By the time most Kenyan children reached adolescence they had grown fluent in two or more languages. And English being the nation's official language, young people thirsted to grasp and speak it. During my Nairobi school months, the moment I tried bumbling through half a sentence of Swahili in the company of a local teen, the youngster had swiftly started a response in crisp, clear English. Practice of the trade language with nationals beyond the classroom was rare.

But I was dead set on communicating well. And, after all, Mwalimu Mzee *insisted.* Textbook-grammar, precise wording, these were my aims. I *must not* yield to the great linguistic transgression — employing *upcountry* Swahili.

But now we'd settled in a place hundreds of miles further inland and my textbook Swahili wasn't faring well. The locals in the countryside couldn't track with me. After all, I had moved *here* now. *Upcountry!*

Maybe time had come to face reality.

I suppose it does make sense. . . What's the purpose of having language, anyway? Oh! to communicate. Painfully weaning myself from squeaky-clean grammar, I made the plunge,

"If you can't beat them, join them."

Once my tongue went the new direction, my words were happily received—faulty pronunciation, scandalous grammar and all.

◊◊◊

"No! SAFARI Ants!"

We shot from either side of our bed —blanket, sheets, pillows flying. Flailing through mosquito netting like flies exiting a bad spider web.

All had been pitch dark in the thatched hut. My wife and I had slept only a couple hours when the flesh-eating troops attacked. "Ouch! Oh! Oh!! Ouch, Ahh!!"

"Jerry, where's the torch?"

"Feeling for it down here at the headboard. Keep moving about! Don't stop moving!" I called, blindly surveying the floor by hand.

"Ah!" The flashlight's narrow beam cut through the black. We kept active, hopping about, grabbing garments.

"Shake your stuff out before putting it on," I called, dancing into my jeans.

Unlatching the door, we scurried outside and up the hill to our host's lodging. Answering our tap-tap at the metal door, our Mennonite friends hurried us in. "Sorry guys," I apologized, "some unexpected visitors chased us out. Otherwise, your guest hut is perfect."

"There's some up here, biting my head." Ann raced her fingers every direction through her hair. Sharon Stutzman sprang to action and soon, under the light of a kerosene lantern, relief came.

The aggressive creatures, sometimes called *army ants*, appeared each rainy season. Moving as if commanded by field lieutenants, they advanced to places where meat was found: human, animal, insect, reptile. Safari ants were not choosey.

Will Burnham, an older Englishman who, with his wife served with us at Bukuria, chuckled once during a visit over tea. Recalling his lightning moves the year before when he shed a pair of infested trousers along some grassy trail.

"Lucky the grass was high, letting me keep some dignity. And you know," he added in a strong Liverpool voice, "when they bite, they hang on for dear life. They won't drop away with a simple brush-off. Aye, you must pick them off, one-by-one."

Experiments led me to an effective trick to block the invaders. Pouring a light trail of paraffin (kerosene) along the outside base of the mission house usually held them at bay.

We learned of one clever family who, when ants approached, simply vacated their place, lodging with friends a distance away as the ants took over their home. Always on the march for more cuisine, Safari Ants don't linger much after scouring a place, devouring all in sight.

Roaches, rats, centipedes, scorpions. . . beware.

Chapter Twenty

RESTRICTED CUISINE

THE ANT INVASION brought to mind another nighttime drama. In 1950, pioneer missionaries at Bukuria station were awakened.

"*Bwana. Kuja! Ona nyoka kubwa sana!*" ("Come, Sir. A Big snake!")

African voices clamored, alerting the white evangelists inside. "Sirs, Come! Snake. Very big!"

Art Dodzweit stirred. Reaching for his rifle and a fist full of shells, he shouted. "Bud, come! Seems a cobra or python has paid us a visit."

In the mid-1940s, friends Bud Sickler and Arthur Dodzweit had boarded ships to Kenya from the U.S. The agency had commissioned them and their new brides — identical twins, Fay and May — to preach, serve where they might and start churches. A government official had notified them of property.

"That hill over there, just in the distance. It's where we've approved land for your mission. Shall we have a look?" The Englishman helping manage the Crown Colony showed the

Yankee newcomers the plot. Papers were drawn up and signed and the missionaries were left to the work.

Narrow creeks and rivers crisscrossed hilly terrain in Kuria country, some boundaries divided by patches of grazing land. Waterways flooded during rainy seasons. Crop-planting rarely got a mention among the cattle-tending Wakuria in their earlier nomadic days.

With much land yet lying undeveloped, one sobering element featured in the Kuria landscape. Slithering pythons lay camouflaged in the region's undergrowth.

They moved about mostly at night stalking small, sometimes larger game. Their big, round eyes and nimble-forked tongue, keenly detected prey. On the night of the snake alert the sky was black. The men tramped the direction shown them.

Art stopped. Movement in the tall grass by his feet sent shivers along his back. The snake lay nearby, no question. A young Kenyan lowered a flashlight. They spotted signs, blotches of tan broken by cream-tinted borders and black outer lines. Slow forward movement. Art tightened his grip on the gun. *A python for sure.*

"Bud, Bud!" Art's tense voice cut into the night. "I'm gonna shoot, Bud!" He squeezed the trigger. The kick of the rifle threw him back a step.

That moment the python's fore-end, several yards out to the left, instantly rose upward from the hit, the high caliber bullet tearing into its midsection.

Bud stood meters away, silent in the dark. A nearby African, gripping a flashlight, caught the image of the huge snake's head meeting eyeball-to-eyeball with Bud Sickler.

Bud gasped and his legs gave way. Going down in a dead faint, the tall red-haired youth missed the final episode of his friend's triumphant snake kill.

As the newest residents of the same mission compound we quickly learned the Python family had not left the neighborhood. Their presence remained a force to be reckoned with.

I never grew a warm place in my heart for serpents. Never acquired the taste. As the sign at Nairobi's Snake Park only half-jokingly cautions, "Tresspassers will be Poisoned."

Growing up on a farm, I was accustomed to watching my step, tromping through high grass. Water Moccasins (Cottonmouths) and a few non-poisonous varieties frequented our pastures and watering ponds. Indeed, a pleasant summer past-time for my brother and me, was picking off the occasional "varmint" with our dad's .22 rifle. But there was a difference between then and now — between this place and that place. The snakes on the Oklahoma farm tended to be shorter. By ten feet or more.

My first meet-up with a python started when a Kuria man entered the mission grounds, pushing his bike up our sloping drive.

"Good morning, Bwana," the tribesman called out. The bike's rear tire appeared low, likely burdened by some merchandise inside the old burlap bag resting atop the carrier rack.

I greeted the stranger and learned he lived nearby – his family occupying two thatch-roofed huts, with a *boma* (home-built corral) sandwiched between.

I eyed the bag with growing curiosity. It was anchored down by strips of discarded inner tube. The man's smile stayed easily in place under his floppy brown hat.

"We Kuria find that missionaries like the skins. The white people coming before you—they pay us shillings for what we bring."

My new-discovered neighbor started undoing the rubber

strips. Heaving the coarse bag to the ground, he untied the thin strand of fresh tree bark used to bind the sack. Slowly he drew out the contents. My eyes widened.

A few minutes of back and forth discussion followed. Pocketing the dollar's-worth of shillings I'd offered, he wheeled the bike around and was gone.

I stared at the python spread full-length before me, its patchwork pattern and its sheer size, a thing of wonder.

How do they skin these things?

I rehearsed the Kuria man's tale of the night just passed.

He had wakened to the screams of one of his goats. It was being seized and encircled by the great serpent. Two gashes in the snake's body revealed where the man's spear struck. More drama followed till the reptile finally lay dead. I never learned the fate of the snake's intended prey but assumed the family would soon dine on goat meat.

Once I skinned my new prize, I spread it full-length on the longest, flattest board available. With small nails securing it, the interior lay stretched open to the sunny sky. Powdering it thoroughly with table salt, I let it rest till it cured.

Reaching to my tool box I found a measuring tape. Nose to tail it stretched 17 feet.

Mid-afternoon I was startled by a sudden cry from my wife outside. She raced toward our first-born. "No, Julie! No, No, don't touch!"

Our 30-month-old daughter had been introduced to the tangy flavor of salt. Spotting the seasoning sprinkled atop a curious thing lying in the open sun, she quickly moved in for direct samples on her extended tongue. Thankfully, Julie's mother interrupted her before she could acquire a taste.

Chapter Twenty-One

GOOD WILL DISCLOSURE

As a foreigner in a region where locals had rarely sighted a light-skinned human, I knew the feeling of *different*. Would the Kuria community come to trust my motives, accept me?

During a season of discouragement, when my best efforts as an outsider to connect with the tribespeople seemed futile, I knelt on the concrete floor in a back room of our house. The prayer was direct, sincere and brief.

"God, please help these people to know I love them."

In the silence an inner voice seemed to interrupt my plea. While it was kind, the voice also came direct, firm.

"*Love* the people. You just love them."

Simple and sparse, like a mail-order kit showing up but without instructions.

How do I do this?

Years afterward a description of *Love* crossed my path. *To will the good of another.* I have yet to hear it better defined.

Through years following I revisited the Bukuria scene. Going to my knees in blue jeans and tee shirt at a location fifteen-hours' drive from where Stanley met Livingstone under a mango tree. I ponder again the response to my prayer that day. *Just love them.*

By now the Africa work had me busy co-authoring a Gospel of John study book, a curriculum piece for *Theological Education by Extension*, widely referred to as *T – E – E.*

"*Mwalimu* (Teacher)," Pastor Mwangi called. He lifted his textbook in a moving gesture . Heartwarming.

"Before you came with the teachings, *Mwalimu* — before bringing us these Bible studies. . . ." Mwangi's voice went softer.

"In those days on a Saturday I would prepare a sermon. But I only knew to follow a certain way. I did not know another way.

"I would pray, then with my eyes closed, bring my Bible open — letting it fall open where it would. I let my finger go to a place there on the page. Opening my eyes, I looked at the place. The words there became my message for Sunday."

"That way I used did not work well but it was all I knew." He shrugged his shoulders. "I did not know another way."

Pastor Mwangi concluded in a reverent tone, as if offering up a sacrament.

"Now I know the good way. Thank you for bringing this Bible School, this T.E.E. I feed my people now and they are helped."

Mounting my bike, I turned toward home — warmed, affirmed in my calling. I thanked God who had willed the good of a tribal people hungry for knowledge, and for him. And who was letting me have a part. *Just loving them.* Together.

◊◊◊

"Now, Jerry", My friend's tone hinted at mischief as we

started across the church parking lot. We were on furlough, and back in Texas "Tell me about *Tee-Hee-Hee.*"

To know Van Gill was to treasure the sound of a rolling chuckle. And to take in a pair of grinning eyes, coaxing response to his merriment.

Everything about the Texan pastor was large. Large frame, large mind (among the keenest), large humor. All these reflecting what was largest of all — his overflowing, over-spacious heart.

Van was a man of the Book. Indeed, it was his love of Scripture that stirred him to offer the teasing invitation. . .*tee-hee-hee.*

Writer's workshops were led by Fred and Grace Holland of the Association of Evangelicals of Africa and Madagascar. They trained missionaries and nationals in Bible school text development.

After my training I partnered with Evangelist Josephat Rungu of Western Kenya. Together, we teamed with South African counterparts and the textbook, *Studies in John* was born. Published in Nairobi, the overall T.E.E. series, featuring topics ranging from *Old Testament Survey* to *Bringing People to Jesus,* spanned denominations and cultures across the continent.

From Latin America to Africa and beyond, *T.E.E.* was empowering the church, equipping spiritual shepherds in the care of their flocks. Especially those pastors and elders who were unable, for various reasons, to access other training. Schools often were traditional schooling in far-away, cultur-ally-detached settings.

When our extension Bible school met weekly under a big tree at mid-day, we engaged a means to dodge the harsh rays. "That's it, bring your chair again this direction. Keep moving ahead of the sun."

Week after week, month after month, young and old apprentices to Jesus engaged each other in such settings. Some indoors, some out. They sipped hot tea, the other hand waving to emphasize a point. Laughter erupted now and then. The minds of these, God's servants, awakened to fresh discovery of truth. They grappled with ancient scripture, sought ways to apply it well. In their own lives, their households, and to the broader community of faith. Their aim? Transformed lives by Jesus and the Holy Spirit.

Through our beloved Africa years, perhaps nothing — apart from watching my three children grow — brought me greater pleasure, more joy.

Tee-hee-hee. Not bad.

————

"See this stone in the path? Now this one too, here in the picture on the same trail. . . ."

I sat with half a dozen men, some a decade or more older than me. The hut we gathered in each week was roofed with long grass. The floor consisted of smooth, hardened dirt. A semicircle of dark benches carried our weight and were worn smooth, long sense having yielded up their last dangling splinter. It was Thursday and one of this week's T.E.E. lessons focused on Jesus visiting with a woman at a water well.

Mature, practical and sincere. These upcountry servants of the church took in the illustration. It struck a chord. Two stumbling-stones: one denoting male pride, the other, tribalism.

Here a woman of a different tribe met Jesus. Sometimes we let the division of tribes hinder God's work. Male pride also hinders. Like big rocks in the pathway that make people stumble. In order to give the good news to the woman, Jesus overcame these two problems.

I reviewed the scene with my African friends.

"See the person Jesus found at the well. A woman speaking with an accent. Of another tribe, a different people."

I studied the men's faces. "Who would like to describe this event? Can you help the rest of us see what good thing Jesus wanted to bring to the woman? What two problems did Jesus point out so she could be helped?"

A pastor nodded. He launched carefully in, reviewed the narrative, raised the matter of how women are at times looked down on, mistreated. The room was quiet. A second leader followed, touching on issues of tribalism, the challenges of going beyond, as Jesus did.

"Can we trust the Lord is with us today? To help us change?"

Heads nodded. Confession voiced by two or three. We prayed.

We left, trusting Jesus as we were able, to lead.

Chapter Twenty-Two

TO SEE MISTER BUCKLEY

"OKAY NOW, STEADY DOES IT."

Leery of the structure's soundness, we stayed crouched on our bellies, crawling forward. Upward, higher on the old roof. A loud crack of splintering wood. We froze.

Bukuria Mission Station rested atop a long sloping hill. Well before our move here, a student dormitory fashioned of sun-baked earth was converted to a house of worship. After years of wear, the *mabati* (corrugated iron sheets) called for replacement.

Phil Harmon, my Canadian friend and a gifted craftsman, showed up to help. We donned carpentry aprons.

"Let's start at this end and work our way to the front, eh?"

Armed with a claw hammer, I followed him up the ladder and the task was underway. Wresting brittle nails from rafters, passing ancient mabati sheets to day-laborers below.

"I guess this lumber under us is OK – you know, sturdy enough – not too termite-eaten?"

Now and then throughout the morning we felt movement. Slight, occasional trembles along the old trusses, our only defense from plummeting downwards. When the roof creaked, we would pause, draw in a slow breath, and proceed.

Finally, the trusses lay uncovered, their purlins denuded, every tin sheet gone. From our perch atop a wall-plate, I took in the scene, "Not bad for a sunny day's work."

Like tight-rope artists, Phil and I made our way to the west end. He paused and stooped. With a gloved hand he casually dislodged a modest piece of two-by-four. Cracking, clapping, thundering collisions of wood followed, like a lumber-yard symphony unleashed. A sound I will never forget.

The whole network of roofing, hundreds and hundreds of rafter and truss feet, gave way. At the frightful sound of lumber splintering apart, our two African helpers below lurched to the side for safety. The crash unleashed a rumbling *boom*. Dust billowed. My Ontario bud and I breathed relief once we spotted the men below still standing – their bodies hugged to the walls – shaken, but unscathed.

Powderpost Beetles, we later discovered, had long been dining on the church's canopy, riddling the lumber with a million pinholes.

In the crash's aftermath, poised above the debris, we silently took in the crisscross of rubbish scattered below. A pile of slightly-bonded sawdust lay there, material upon which we had entrusted our weight throughout the day.

At last Phil turned. He released a low chuckle, "Looks like we're spared having to take apart the frame."

"Yeah, and I think a couple guardian angels got in some overtime today."

◊◊◊

"George'll do it."

The phrase sprang to life across East Africa in the 70's. Repeated often by a string of newbie missionaries, "George'll do it" stayed current through the decade and into the next. We and other youthful couples were deepening our ministry roots across the region.

Seating myself near a side table at the mission house fireplace, I reached for the radio call transmitter, pressed the thumb button, and began, "2098, 2098 – this is Radio Call 2-0-9-8 – Come in, George, come in. Over." Voiceless static greeted me. I waited. More attempts followed, some stretching past a quarter hour. I pressed on. Finally, a crackle. Then a distant, but familiar voice, "Yes. George, here. Hi, Jerry. Over."

Hundreds of miles from the city and no phone service between, the lofty transmitter tower out front of the station home meant a lifeline to civilization.

George and June Lindsay served in the capital city. As Elim's Field Secretary, George stayed alert for calls – routine and urgent – from the many apprentices under his charge. More than a mere *go-fer* (running impromptu errands from fetching car parts to government paper-work), George *pastored* us. Modeling servanthood.

A gentle giant-in-the-making, George embodied a principle: The Lord doesn't pursue merely *gifted* people. He goes after *available* people.

This quality in George is traced to his first response to an overseas call. When a mission's recruiter challenged, "The Bukuria station is hurting for someone to join the team, and the need is urgent."

The appeal was hardly voiced, when young George piped up, "I can hammer nails. I'll go." Years later, his sister, Shirley

May Davis, penned a biography. With a fitting title, "Servant Shoes".

◊◊◊

Our little girl joined her mother in outings to Kehancha market.

"Mommy, that's Bhoke and her sister, Robi. There's my friend Mwita with his Uncle Chacha." Julie leaned out the car window, waving, "Hi Mwita, Hi Mzee Chacha!" it seemed our three-year-old knew every name in the tribe. Smiling large, they waved back.

"Jerry, we should leave for the city soon. I've confirmed our room at *the Mennonite*." Ever the keen planner, Ann was eager to get to Nairobi. Arrival of baby-number-two drew near. We earlier set a buffer period to spare us a potential hasty six-hour delivery drive.

Of the city's handful of guest houses, *the Mennonite* was our favorite. When we rolled up in our Beetle, the matron, Mrs. Hostetter, welcomed us. An alluring fragrance from the kitchen area wakened our taste buds. The kind hostess, her small circular head-piece in place, excused herself, "Dinner is at 6:00. Enjoy your stay."

A couple days in, Ann stirred.

"Honey, we'd better get going. I believe it's time."

Reaching for her small apple-red suitcase, I called back, "Okay, babe. Here we go!"

Late that evening a nurse moved to my wife's bedside. "Mister Buckley will see you and your fine little boy early morning, Mrs. Lout."

We were growing accustomed, by now, to a curious practice in the world of British medicine. Where a fully-certified specialist gets his title elevated from "Doctor" up to "Mister."

Ann found Mister Buckley's check-up visits always informative and professional.

By the time our third baby, Amy, broke through to the light of a delivery room, I had been alongside my wife in pre-birthing hours with each child. By some miracle, satisfactorily aiding their mother with breathing routines through most of the contractions. The supreme highlight — witnessing each precious life emerge well, then hearing them squall with everything in them. Sweet sounds of life.

In the Africa of the 1970's post-delivery care meant a lengthy time of bedrest. A week after Scott Timothy made his loud entry to the world, he and his mother were freed to leave Nairobi Hospital. By then every nurse and several of the other new moms had held him close.

The four of us made the long drive home, only to revisit Nairobi Hospital in a mere six weeks for a critical surgery.

Chapter Twenty-Three

MACHETE ALARM

KLAK. Klak. Klak. Klak.

The sound of an archery bow thumping a bedroom window after midnight is not easily forgotten.

Our night watchman's smokie voice sounded his wakeup call, pronouncing my last name as best he could, "Bwana Lauti, Bwana Lauti."

At Nyamahanga's second or third call, I stirred. My bedside clock read 1:30 a.m.

"Bwana Lauti. . . Mama *karibu kuzaa.*"

The cement-plaster floor of our room felt cool to my bare feet. Flashlight in hand, I moved to the door. "Honey, another ambulance run. A Kuria Mama's gone into labor."

"Okay," a sleepy voice murmured back. "Be careful." It was a role reversal for Ann, the frequent late-night riser when a baby needed changing or fed.

Ten minutes passed. I whispered a prayer as the father-to-be who had raised the alert, took his place in the passenger seat. We were off to fetch the missus, then get her to Kehancha.

Such "ambulance runs" evolved as part of a naturally-assumed job description for any bush missionary. The assumption made sense as mission personnel were among the scant number of people who owned a car. The race against time came pantingly close, but we somehow outpaced the labor contractions in each of the mostly late night jaunts.

My friend, Phil, of nearby *Suna Mission* didn't fare so well. A good part of the morning found him in vigorous scrub-down mode of the floorboard and rear seat of his freshly-christened *VW Delivery Room*. Mother and newborn fared well.

Over time we grew to wonder what next crisis could visit the compound. It was during such a period a young man appeared at our back entrance. He bled profusely, leaning into the support of another man.

The machete attack had found its mark. *Jesus help us.*

◊◊◊

The young pastor strained under the weight of the bleeding man. "He is my brother." He labored to keep the wounded man upright. The machete blade had gone deep.

"How did it happen?" I asked. My wife entered from a side room, prompting in me a silent *thank God for her nurse's training.*

"My brother has a friend. The friend sent my brother to collect money owed him by another man."

We helped move the wounded brother out of his coat, its fabric soaked through in red.

"The man owing money was drinking beer and angry when my brother told him why he came. My brother decided to leave and come back another time. But the man had taken up a panga (machete). When my brother turned to go out, it was then he was slashed, before he could reach to the outside."

Ann brought out a sizable roll of gauze. By now his shirt had been removed. With strips of old sheets and tape, she bound his bare torso. The panga had opened a V-trench some eight inches long — vertically, between spine and shoulder blade. She wrapped the material about him several times, hoping it might slow the blood. We had to buy time to get him to the clinic where they could sew him up.

The government-sponsored clinic, a thinly-equipped medical outpost established to serve the local clans, sat at the edge of the village nearest us.

Life was hard for the tribal people, often heartbreaking. It was a rare home that had not lost at least one child to malaria.

And there were the skirmishes.

With cultures of the region given to decades-old feuds – mostly over livestock – violence could erupt in a heartbeat. Kuria country bordered other cattle-tending families. Bands of spear-wielding parties of either tribe trekked by foot to take back rustled livestock.

I slowed the *Beetle* down on our dusty road. Rolled gently past the occasional vigilante parties. We couldn't guess when a band might come into view on the twenty-mile drive to our mail box. As a missionary family we did not feel directly threatened, but our verbal charge to back seat passengers came with regularity, "Roll your windows up, kids."

The task at hand was to transport a terribly wounded young Kuria for treatment. I hoped the doctor was in.

"Sir. . . Sirrr, Hello. . . Hello! Can you come sir? Hello. . . ."

Waking a physician from a drink-induced sleep called for persistence.

We transported the machete-attack victim the five miles to

the government clinic. But an aged, slow-moving male nurse was the only person on duty.

"The doctor for this kind of work," he said, eyeing the wide blood-mark down our patient's back, "is away. You might find him at his house."

Leaving our patient, I drove another five miles of bad road, where I came to the darkened home of the doc. "Hello. . .Hello. . . ."

Thirty minutes later, the groggy doc held a kerosene lantern (electricity had not reached the village) and examined the naked wound. Thankfully, Ann's gauze-and-sheet wrap had held. Not much blood had seeped through.

The wounded man went by *Mwita.* He sat upright on the cot's edge as we gazed at the deep slash. I had never seen such a wound.

No surgical mask was donned. There were none in supply. Maybe never had been.

A brief exchange with the bush-surgeon left me troubled. The nurse had stepped to another room and was now rolling in a metal cart. A steel pan and utensils with suturing material, I guessed.

My tone was respectful. "Sir, could I ask. . . what is used to sterilize the instruments?"

Lifting a large curved needle offered by the old nurse, the gentleman held it to the lantern for a better look. With a wave of an elbow he declared, "In the big cities where many people live, they have a lot more germs. Many more.

"But out here in the rural places, we have fewer people. So, less problems with infection." He squinted one-eyed, found the needle's opening and began the thread.

Simply the way it was. No discussion.

I cringed at my next discovery. "He will be given anesthetic, right?" I ventured.

"No, we are out of it."

The needle pierced the muscular surface, tugging a string of black thread in its trail. Again, and again. The sight left me near the edge of nausea.

Next morning, I readied myself to visit the clinic when word of the wounded man reached me via Africa's reliable grapevine.

"You're sure?" I asked a second time.

"Yes, Bwana. He walked home this morning."

I was feeling queasy again.

While missionaries are not widely known for referencing Charles Darwin, I found myself suddenly recalling a phrase, "Survival of the fittest."

Chapter Twenty-Four

TRIPLE TRAUMA

I HAD SHUT the kerosene flow to the lanterns and, as typical on a Bukuria Mission night, we had fallen asleep by 11 p.m. For an hour, all was quiet.

Ann's cry of pain shocked me awake.

"Honey, what's wrong? What *is* it?"

My dear wife had bolted upright, seizing her midsection. The pain was searing. A few frightening moments then the surge of agony eased.

Ann previously had a flare-up like this, but not nearly so severe.

Soon as arrangements were made, our little foursome headed once more for Nairobi. Ann's doctor in the capital had figured an inflamed gall bladder was the culprit.

Wearied by the trip, of trailing behind smoke-belching buses and lorries at varying intervals along the two-lane road, we pulled in to the Maxwell's home in South C. Ann would go in for surgery the next morning. A day we would never forget.

November 20, 1974. As the hour-hand of the Nairobi hospital clock struck eight a.m., a Lufthansa Jumbo Jet sped along a runway. The flight marked the final segment of a Frankfurt – Nairobi – Johannesburg route. Seconds later, barely airborne, the aircraft dropped to earth. Its tail broke apart. As the left wing exploded, fire spread to the fuselage.

A tragic day in aviation history for the East African nation. No airplane mishap in Kenya has brought more fatalities. Fifty-nine of the 157 passengers and crew died. Many others suffered injuries, some with severe burns. It was the first-ever 747 crash resulting in lives lost. The cause: insufficient air lift due to mechanical settings.

"We will reschedule you, Mrs. Lout, once we learn more. At present, our staff are on alert for casualties arriving from the crash."

Remarkably, Ann was called in for surgery the following morning. After the gall-bladder removal she was granted permission to have our nursing son join her in the private room.

Our prayers these days carried a range of emotion. Heaviness for the bereaved and the injured of Flight 540, relief and thankfulness our family could journey again soon. Back to our upcountry home.

◊◊◊

The mission doctor drew his penlight back from my little girl's ear and sent me a sympathetic look.

His voice betrayed a strong Dutch accent, "The infection is bad."

The young doc had recently been assigned to *Ombo* clinic, a Catholic mission outpost in Migori village. I had brought three-year-old Julie in, hoping to remedy her nonstop earache. Julie sat astride my dirt bike's gas tank during the twenty-mile ride. *Was it wise exposing her head, especially her ears, to the breeze?* A little late to ponder about that.

The physician reached for a sharp-pointed instrument I had no interest seeing.

"I need to pierce the ear drum, and you'll want to hold her firm."

What followed was one of the necessary and least welcome assignments presented parents of young children. How to explain piling pain on top of pain at the hands of the white-coated man whose job was to bring pain's relief. And at the hands of Daddy, whose likeness was akin to a deity.

Why Daddy? Why do you help this man hurt me? My daughter's distressed eyes begged the answer more pressing than her voice ever could.

I swallowed hard, my fear rising from the insecurity of youthful fatherhood. *I was never schooled in this thing going on here.* I hoped my voice carried confidence, "It's okay, sweetheart. It'll be okay soon."

My greater struggle came from within rather than from the physical act of imprisoning my princess in a smothering hold.

Mercifully, the sharp pierce of the surgeon's device came and went quickly. Julie's sudden cry cut through the lab facility, echoing harshly in the uncarpeted, brick-walled room. The whimpers soon trailed off as she grew calm. I rocked her slowly back and forth. The infectious throbbing went away, the pounding pain gone. Her tense body relaxed. She quieted.

Years afterward, the visit to Ombo Clinic prompted me to reflect. Of God's most-recognized titles, "Father" must rank the highest.

Thank you, Lord, that when I least understand you or your actions, your care and wisdom and presence get me past my confusion and pain. Eventually.

Every time.

Chapter Twenty-Five

THE CHASE

I HAD NEVER SET eyes on a spitting cobra. Not up close, not uncaged. And certainly not mere steps from my children's sand box.

"Mpiga, Mpiga (stone it, stone it)!" Cries of twenty voices shattered the mission station's quiet. The children had come upon the snake while heading home, taking their usual short cut across the mission property.

Swinging our back door open, I took in the spectacle from the veranda. "Looks like the school kids got a varmint in their sights, hon."

At this point the serpent had not moved into my view. On the other hand, every clamoring adolescent traced the snake's moves. It slithered through foot-high grass, barely ahead of the children's hail of ammo, stones and sticks raining down.

The moment the cobra got near our lawn, I shouted, "Rafel!" The muscular day-laborer rushed toward my voice. Seeing the danger to our children — to all of us — he raced to a nearby tree, a hefty machete in his grip. In seconds a tree limb plopped to the ground. Rafel alighted. *Whack, whack,*

whack. He soon displayed an impressive weapon, long enough to go after the cobra. *But can he dodge its venomous spray?*

Although our children were safely indoors with their mom, a chill shot through me as one of Africa's most feared creatures suddenly swung about to face me. I shivered, freshly aware my children's sandbox lay two meters away.

The forebody of the snake rose thirty inches off the ground. It spread wide its gray hood and shot a toxic stream at the worker and me, thankfully short of its targets. Spotting the entryway to an abandoned chicken coop, it moved inside.

With more tension than either Rafel or I wished to claim, we guardedly shoved the door aside. Again, the cobra's head swung our direction. The snake moved from the far end of the little coop straight toward us, its speed fueled by the panic that drives any creature feeling trapped. We leapt aside.

When the reptile rose again to spread its hood, Rafel was ready. The thick end of his club crashed to the snake's head.

The primary school kids cheered wildly. Finally, they quieted and dispersed, chattering as they covered the distance to their thatch and tin-roofed dwellings.

The drama ended. I took little interest in Cobras or in cobra skins. My curing plank would lie undisturbed, even for this seven-footer. It was enough for my wife and me that our preschoolers were safe. That the four of us would dine together that night, undisturbed.

Chapter Twenty-Six

FAMILIES ON MISSION

"AUTUMN! Pull your pants up, right this minute!"

When eight pre-school children of four young missionary couples (two M.K.s per household) suddenly go quiet in their outdoor play, the angst of parents rises. An observation by a young woman whose tone of voice belies a motherly instinct, "Hey guys, anyone notice the kids aren't making any sounds?"

The occasion was our mission's area meeting, convened every couple months for food, sharing, prayer.

Devotional reflections, prayer requests among the grownups trailed off. Apprehensions stirred, gradually at first. Imaginations fired up, *We're in Black Mamba country (Africa's deadliest snakes). If the children have wandered off to the trees. . . .*

Little Autumn's father stepped across the living room and quietly peered out an elevated window. He took in our missing company of eight urchins. They stood in a circle beneath a Frangipani tree at the house's edge. Each in turn, surveyed from a reasonable distance what they could of one another's lower anatomy.

The mothers sprang for the outside doors. They and the other adults had, seconds before, entered a quiet moment of prayer. So much for that.

In days following, parents regaled one another with follow-up snippets.

"Son, did you have your pants down out there before the others?"

"No, Mommy." Mark seemed dismayed. "I tried but couldn't get them to unbutton."

Another of the moms, Sarah, noting the useful role humor carries in the sometimes-strained work of international missions, voiced a nugget of wisdom, "He who laughs lasts."

◊◊◊

"And why have you come to this country?" The Kenyan official eyed the two passports, each bearing the surname Kingsbury. From beyond the terminal the roar of another passenger jet touching down.

"We have come to serve as missionaries."

Studying the couple an extra second, his rubber stamp poised, the official offered, "You're too young to be missionaries." Chip and Chari breathed a sigh as the stamp thump-thumped each document.

"Okay, guys," I called out as we gathered luggage, "next stop — a wedding!"

After the July 4th ceremony the happy and weary newly-weds made their way home.

Moses and Jacinta pressed into pastoral work. Funds were tight but they never drew back from the throb of mission they had embraced. His open-air meetings at the city market entrance – teaching, mentoring, lifting, challenging – fueled an increase. Of new believers, and of laborers alike. As the couple brought children of their own into the world, the Holy Spirit added sons and daughters to the believing community.

And as more locals, many of them recent converts, offered themselves in service, the cry for training grew.

"Here we are, Jerry, all the extension materials accounted for." The Kingsbury's joining us in the Nyeri work came at the right time. Our friendship deepened. Christian workers caught vision, increased their knowledge, prayed fervently, grew bold. The Lord's kingdom expanded.

"Okay kiddos, let's see what the Pevensies and Aslan are up to today!" Nothing fired up our children's imagination (nor our own) like the weekly Tuesday ritual with Uncle Chip. Reading aloud, one by one, all seven volumes of C.S. Lewis's *Chronicles*.

Coming years saw Sunday Schools launched as Ann and Chari trained African volunteers eager to nurture children in Scripture. Effective objects lessons for installing truth were fashioned of raw materials within easy reach. A pile of pebbles, a thorny plant, maize seed. Young Pastor Moses poured heart and soul into the Pentecostal Evangelistic Fellowship of Africa, a work springing from Elim's earlier vision. Regardless the labels, Christ had gained a hearing.

Sipping chai alongside X-ray tech Haniel and Civil servant Hector, I watched the T.E.E. trainees apply Biblical truths to hard problems. Their tackling real issues by prayer and obedience deepened confidence, increased their spiritual influence. Powerful change affected through ordinary and not-so-ordinary Jesus-followers. Fallible, limping, *works-in-progress*.

"Where's that bird?"

Missionary playtimes meant good-natured banter, table

games and food aplenty. A deck of ROOK cards with the Schwandt's, accompanied by Irv's mimicked bird trills, an uncanny likeness to the real thing. Our harmonizing barbershop pieces often followed, while the unimpressed spouses rolled their eyes.

The Kingsburys, Pastor Moses, the Schwandts, and myriad other servants leave their marks across the continent, and the world. The face of Christ. Rescuing. Equipping. Commissioning still others into ready-ripened vineyards.

Chapter Twenty-Seven

THE SWARM

WHEELING the car onto the dusty grounds of Kehancha Clinic, my latest patient on board, I took in a distressing sight. A little girl not yet two cried pitifully. The weary mother held her, laboring in vain to quiet the child's recurring wails.

These and others made up a still-gathering line of ill and injured awaiting their turn for treatment, assuming meds were available. The group, most strangers to each other, sat on a shallow wooden bench butted against the clinic's outside wall. Bare spots in the building's whitewashed veneer marked areas where chunks of old plaster had finally released their hold.

My attention returned to the small child, her eyes clamped as if glued shut. Her face ballooned, a tormented ball of puff.

I never learned the child's fate, just a snippet of what brought her to the clinic. A swarm of bees descended with no warning from upper branches of a tree. Her older siblings fled in panic, leaving the little one as the bee's lone target.

Killer Bees. A term suited to theatre marquees promoting the latest horror film. Some years after the distressing scene outside the clinic, a ferocious swarm nearly cost a friend his life.

"Ray, what's going on with the dogs? Sounds like they've gone crazy." Ray moved near his wife by the window. They witnessed their two beloved German Shepherds in a yelping frenzy. Crying, barking. Without a pause, Ray rushed out. Margaret watched as he raced across the open farm yard, then looked on in horror as an enormous swarm blanketed the animals and her husband.

As Ray flailed at the attackers with one hand, he worked frantically to free the dogs of their running-leashes. "Come Princess!"

But the dog lay motionless, heavy against Ray's hard tug, already a casualty to the angry swarm.

The battle had only begun.

The migrating African breed terrorized regions throughout the year, sweeping onto their victims without mercy.

Her husband raced to the sanctuary of his house. "Marge, grab cushions, a pillow! Beat me! Knock the bees off!" Ray was tall, athletic, fit. But the African bees had gone after his six-foot, seven-inch frame in a vicious frenzy.

Slamming the front door behind her husband, Margaret pounded pillows against him. Buzzing attackers dropped to the floor while others clung to his arms, his neck and face. His bared legs below khaki shorts were darkened by scores of bees. Still others moved about his hair and clothing.

When he raced through the doorway, Ray had been carrying a yelping bundle of fur— their youngest canine, small and lovable. Marge drew water into a tub and threw in the insect-covered pup. Bees fell away. The whimpering, drenched animal would likely be saved.

With a strange wooziness now overtaking her husband,

Marge labored to get him past a second doorway and into their dusty-white Peugeot station wagon.

Ray sat half-slumped in the passenger seat. The car raced along the winding drive and onto the Nakuru highway, an anxious and prayerful Marge at the wheel. They sped the ten kilometers toward the nearest decent clinic. Even with her gas pedal nearly touching the floorboard, the race-track speed of the station wagon felt more like a crawl.

An open gateway came into view. "At last," Marge breathed.

Gravel flew amid a swirl of dust. She braked the car to a hard stop at the clinic's entrance.

Ray seemed to weaken with each second. Deadly toxins mingled in his bloodstream and Marge knew he was fading. Laboring to escort him toward the clinic door, she whispered, "Jesus, let there be time. Please Jesus."

Chapter Twenty-Eight

THIN PLACES

"STUNG! BEE STINGS! STUNG BY BEES!"

The words tripped over each other, as Marge called to a nurse while steadying her woozy husband. Desperation turned to near-panic. She caught the sympathetic nurse's response, her East African English clear, crisp.

"I am sorry, ma'am. The doctor has gone out. He should be back soon."

A moment's pause. Marge wheeled about. "Ray, we can't wait. We have to get help now!"

They had moved just a few steps outside when the resident doctor rounded the clinic's corner, meeting the disheveled couple face-to-face. A rush of relief swept over Marge. Taking in a short breath, she spilled out the critical details.

The doctor's action was swift, decisive. He whisked Ray back inside.

"Quickly!" Doctor Mwangi's orders came clipped, strong and no less commanding than if barked by a military officer.

"We'll get you onto this table, Mister Ray." A glance toward Marge, "Let's ease him to his back please."

Marge aided the understanding physician, noting both his urgency and professionalism.

Soon a syringe was in hand. He held it up, eyes and palm in synchronized union. "Mister Ray, this antivenom should help once it's in."

But Ray had gone quiet.

Marge caught a troubled look clouding the doctor's face.

Agonizing moments followed, snailing by, second-on-second as she gazed tensely at her husband's still form. The needle found its mark. Antibodies flowed. Suddenly Ray's chest lifted. *He's taking in air.*

The big man's eyes fluttered.

Ancient Christian writers spoke of a place, a curious, mystical kind of place. Elusive. But a real place. A zone where the immediate presence of the spirit world, though seldom detected, could appear – for some moments at least – very close.

So close, in fact, that hardly a distinction is made. A to and fro over a divide, an intermingling of the physical world we are accustomed to and the mystical or invisible world. A place beyond and yet at hand. Spiritual sages knew it as the "thin place."

A few weeks after Ray's ordeal we met up, "Jerry, you've heard of a thing called an 'out of body' experience, right?"

"Yeah." I lifted an eyebrow.

"That was me, bro. . . that was *me*."

He had my attention.

"Yeah, really. There in the clinic.

"Lying there on my back before the doc's needle went in, I sensed myself rising. Yes, I *was* rising. But my body was *not*. My body just lay there, still. I know because I saw it. Soon I was up somewhere near the room's ceiling, man. . . looking down on the scene." He paused, revisiting the setting.

"The thing only lasted seconds. When the needle went into my vein and the meds took hold, I was instantly back." Ray drove home the point with a single clap of his big hands.

"Before that though, for a few seconds I guess, I was watching everything from above." His head cocked upward.

". . . Watching the doc. . . seeing Marge. . . seeing *me* — my body — yeah, me. Seeing myself just lying there. Surreal!"

By the time my friend left the clinic to return home, some 130 stingers had been extracted from his body.

The mission family and other friends thanked God and celebrated. The pleadings and speedy action of a praying wife had prevailed.

Ray came back.

Chapter Twenty-Nine

ALTERING VISITS

THE MID-TWENTIETH-CENTURY TSUNAMI sweeping inland from the coastal town of Mombasa carried with it no carnage, no loss of lives. . . no water. What the wave of spiritual awakening brought was a movement of transformed cultures. Among Kenyans, Ugandans and Tanzanians for years to come.

The voice boomed, "Only the power of the living Christ proclaimed in demonstration of the Holy Spirit can meet the urgent needs of humanity."

Oklahoma-born evangelist T. L. Osborn launched his Gospel crusade in Kenya's second largest city on the shores of the Indian Ocean. It was 1957.

The message of Christ was preached. Prayers for healing followed. Africans yielded to Christ in large numbers, many gaining freedom from sicknesses, others from addictions and crippling lifestyles.

Once the series of meetings ended, the message of Christ continued sweeping inland through the service of compassionate and emboldened men and women.

According to one African churchman, the Mombasa meetings released the fountain of a river spreading through the heart of East Africa. Hundreds of new believers launched overnight as Gospel preachers throughout the region. Most did so with slim if any funding, scant organizational backing and, of course, little Biblical training. Within a few years, thousands of new churches had sprung up in bustling cities and sleepy villages.

It was into this sudden birth of new churches the generation of missionaries ahead of ours had landed. Most of us who followed had finished Bible school but lacked maturity born from experience in life and ministry. Two or three training schools had opened in the region by now, but the demand for foundational instruction among hundreds of spiritual shepherds was daunting. Still, we went to work, and a merciful Lord met us there in our frailties.

From Lake Victoria's Luo-land to the Ocean's Mijikenda peoples, African preachers relied on the Holy Spirit, delivered their message, courageously, compassionately. Whole populations, formerly claimed by witchcraft and curses, incantations and the great dread of dying, came alive in the Gospel.

Lyrics of a Swahili chorus gave testament to Holy Spirit encounters: *Moto umeshuka* (Fire fell on me).

The wonder of Christ-centered outbreaks traced to "Spirit-outpourings" was not new to the continent. In the 1920s an African national, Simeon Nsibambi and a missionary, Joe Church, labored together in prayer as they searched Scripture and their own hearts. Both thirsted for holy and empowered living. Others joined in. By the coming decade, waves of sorrow over sin, confession and deliverance, swept across Rwanda and Burundi, Uganda and beyond.

Turning from their wrongs, inviting God's infilling, large

sectors of tribal peoples embraced freedoms they had never known. Love of neighbor and regard for right living displaced crippling practices of the past.

The movement grew. Its transformative impact on religious sectors, educators and households of all descriptions flourished. The movement bore lasting fruit and gained the label, the *East Africa Revival.*

The steady commitment of Africa's preachers and educators recalled a well-known aim often applied to such laborers: *To know Christ and to make Him known.*

Chapter Thirty

BRANCHING OUT

SUNDAY CHURCH SERVICE in the shade of a fruit tree offered its perks.

When a high-up branch at our quaint meeting place let go its grip on a ripened mango, thumping the head of a half-sleeping listener, my Bible class came alive. For the moment anyway.

Mzee Kunda (my Tanzania co-worker) and I had scouted Moshi town in hopes of marking out a preaching point and eventually establishing a church. The spot of land with a mango tree caught our attention.

Kunda, an aging, never-married Chaga tribesman of Kilimanjaro, had endeared himself to great numbers of people as a travelling evangelist. His one-on-one chats brought many across the region, town and country dwellers alike, to a vital faith. From Moshi to Arusha and back, village after village engaged the winsome personality that was Mzee Kunda. He knew his calling and trekked hundreds of miles, facing tough opposition at times, but pressing on to share his compelling messages.

"Mzee," I posed one day, "could you check an area over near the Muslim sector — you know, where the city has no church at all?"

The property he selected was the right size but lacked electricity and water. A small river (all but dry except for the rainy season) snaked nearby. Visits with the land owner brought a meeting of the minds. Prayers went up. Funds came in. We were underway.

"Here young lady, let me steal that freckle." To every feigned reach for her nose by Uncle Dan, Amy offered a grinning giggle. Raising eight daughters of their own, newly-arrived co-workers Dan and Nancy Larkin, came perfectly-skilled for grandparenting our seven-year-old. Excitement stirred in the Kili region when Dan launched a school project on our two-acre grounds. Lazaro Kiriama of Maasai-land entered later to nurture the training center to a thriving ministry, equipping church leaders across the region.

Meanwhile a familiar old tree — like a quiet, loyal friend — shifted its role. From thumping Sunday worshippers with mango missiles, to treating a parade of ministry trainees her juicy delights.

Chapter Thirty-One

A BREAKING

MISSION FIELD TRAUMA can take many forms. Anguish of soul can prove the most severe.

Shutting my eyes a moment, I agonized the fresh image in my mind. More than haunting, the scene of the stricken child consumed my senses.

I stood behind the rough-hewn pulpit looking out at twenty worshippers. A shudder gathered in my back, then up and across my shoulders. How could this have happened? How could I have driven away, on to my precious commitment?

Commitment. The word rang hollow. The reality was, I had left the child, his small body sprawled lifeless on the roadway. It didn't matter that another vehicle hit him. Nor that another stopped. I had driven on. I had left him there, along with his delirious mother.

Although I had lived in Africa for years, the events of that morning counted among my most wrenching. Carnage on the roadways was painfully common. I had come upon more highway wrecks — some utterly gruesome — in our first six months than in all my past years.

Still, I could not divorce myself from this morning's scene. Even as I read Scripture to the gathered faithful and began to speak, the image replayed like a horror scene, rolling its condemning tape through my soul.

The hit-and-run motorist had evidently slowed, then sped out of sight. Moments afterward, I approached. Seeing the child — apparently lifeless — I slowed my truck and steered it partly off the pavement.

A frantic, hysterical young woman in her lovely Sunday dress faced the highway, only feet from the fallen boy. Her eyes were pleading. In that moment, an impulse stirred and, in a move I would have never dreamed myself capable of, I yielded. It was the religious component that made the act not just pathetic, but callous. Repulsive.

We need to get to the meeting. I'm to speak this morning.

As if to dismiss the real-life crisis playing out directly before me, I glanced at my watch. I touched the accelerator and motored on.

Standing at the pulpit now, I felt I was aging.

Never mind that another vehicle *did* stop to lend aid — a fact I had witnessed through my rear-view mirror.

What does that say, Jerry? Compassionate action through a rear-view mirror? Right. Accusing words, in quick succession, flooded in.

The facts were obvious. Severely so. In the face of immediate human need, I had chosen reason over compassion, rationale above mercy.

Another car had stopped, the gray Land Rover, I reasoned.

On the other hand — I, the missionary en route to a preaching appointment — had driven on. Me, with my Sunday church duty to perform.

A soft groan settled in my gut.

Robotically, I shared scripture of a ready-prepared theme. My sermon ended and I soon left the mountain village for home. Sunday mercifully fell behind me.

But on Monday —then into following weeks — I felt haunted. Finally, I questioned, *Will my soul one day recover from the shame bearing down, the humiliation of religion-bred dereliction?*

Bouts of self-loathing continued. That I allowed meetings to trump mercy.

And who needs mercy now? Will it come to me?

Reviewing the roadside scene for the hundredth time, I doubted.

The prophet assures of comfort, *"His compassions fail not"* (Lamentations 3:22).

But is even the mercy of God equal to something like this?

For years after, I questioned. Confessed once again. And again.

I had been given, at my own hand, a teaching moment of a severe kind. Any reference to the Good Samaritan brought a stab. If I were a character in Jesus's famous parable, I was anyone but the generous passerby lending aid. No, I was one of the other guys. Preoccupied. Dutifully religious. Hurrying to my assigned post.

Over time I allowed grace an entrance and, gradually, healing. With God's aid I willed myself to lift the haunting images, along with their pain, repeatedly. Openly up to him. To his cross.

Interior questions verbalized in one way or other. Among the more probing, *How can a string of roadway tragedies witnessed over time so desensitize a man to human suffering?*

The most vital questions surfaced from deep inside. Only

by answering them rightly could relief finally come, *Do I find closure? Do I embrace mercy?*

In time the voice of self-loathing quieted enough that I caught a whispered message, as a merciful intervention. God spoke in a tone I could not expect — surprisingly tender.

He had been whispering all along, but I had muffled his voice by my own self-accusing chorus. His response to my inquiries now came themselves as questions.

"Was my mercy withheld from my servant-king who defiled a man's wife then murdered him to cover his wrong?

"Was my fisherman-friend who three times in succession disowned me, not handed the keys of my kingdom?

"Has not a parade of followers who have offended, failed and incurred shame been welcomed, embraced and celebrated upon returning home, as was the prodigal long ago?"

More questionings followed, tender but firm. Through his questionings, his further whisperings, healing seeped in.

In the end I offered the one response he waited for. I yielded to grace.

"Thank you, Lord. Thank you. Thank you, Father."

Chapter Thirty-Two

NOMAD STIRRING

"WHEN THE *SIMBA* came at me I raised my shield, but then he knocked me back." The young African opened his palm, extending it my way. I surveyed the seasoned lion-claw scar running near his thumb and forefinger. "My brothers then speared him."

The tall lean Maasai named Gaddiel recounted his lion-hunting venture — a tribal rite initiating one to warrior status. His voice was calm, undramatic, as if he were relating details of a routine walk to the local market.

Gaddiel Nkarrabali was now a warmly-regarded Christian pastor among his nomadic, cattle-tending kin. His Gospel work came about in large part because of Eva.

Eva, single missionary mother — her two children schooling at Rift Valley Academy — had come to Kenya in the 60s. They settled in a dusty remote outpost called Mashuru. Her first house, put up in less than two days, was a home-made tin structure covering 209 square feet. Once erected, she and a local co-worker lady settled down for the night.

In her memoir, In The Shadow of Kilimanjaro, Eva relates her next-morning surprise.

"All around the (parked) car were large pad tracks where a lion had inspected it. Well, what you don't see doesn't hurt you. It excited us but we weren't really troubled. We knew what country we were in so went on fixing our little house. . . ."

Along the way the gutsy pioneer missionary came across a young tribal warrior. Gaddiel.

"I had asked some young Morani (warriors) if any would like to go for more schooling." The school in Eva's thinking was Kaimosi Bible School off to the west. None of these young men were Christ-followers.

"Up went a hand. 'Nanu' (I wish to). His name was Gaddiel, the chief of his manyatta (household)."

Years later the cattle-herder turned Christian shepherd, recounted his first days in Bible college.

"I saw many miracles God showed me. One night I prayed so much, asking Jesus to see his face. That very night there came a man in my dream in a great light. I woke up shaking. A song came into my heart. I am sure Jesus was doing something in me. . . ."

"Welcome kiddos!" Eva Butler's cheery greeting at our first arrival to Kenya hadn't yielded a hint that a frontier missionary of giant caliber had entered our world.

◊◊◊

Denny turned sideways in the aircraft seat just enough for me to catch his voice above the engine hum. His words brought sweat to my palms.

The missionary pilot had directed the aircraft toward a volcanic region above East Africa's plains. The Cessna appeared as a baby fly against the backdrop of the continent's most stunning monument, Mount Kilimanjaro.

We had lifted off from Moshi's small airport, bound for five remote preaching outposts. Each outpost was marked by a small gathering of Maasai huddled under one or two trees or beneath a tin roof indicating a village schoolroom.

Denny's passengers also numbered five. Loaded to capacity, we were airborne.

"Every three weeks or so I fly young evangelists to these outposts, leaving them one by one at each preaching point," Denny had said when inviting me along. "They share with any locals who want to learn about God. I offer a teaching at the final spot on the circuit. Afterward, I return home, retracing the earlier route, collecting the evangelists once again on the way." Going by air cut travel time by days.

We had touched down and taken off twice when my French pilot friend clued me in on details of our next landing site.

"Up ahead at that range of peaks, we land on a different kind of strip."

Even from this distance, the landscape appeared varied. It merged with steep green slopes, revealing spherical volcanic outlines. Nothing of the terrain hinted at flatness. As we flew on, several sharp bumps alerted us to updrafts. We drew near one of Africa's towering escarpment cliffs.

The pilot's accented narrative continued, "We approach soon the most difficult landing strip I visit in all the region."

My palms moistened now, despite Denny's steady, casual manner. My imagination engaged, *what does "most difficult landing strip" actually mean, for Denny — for me — today?*

He seemed in a mood to offer more detail than I cared to know. "First, the terrain near this village has no really suitable place for landing a plane, so the length of the strip is quite short. Then the landing and take-off space lies slanted a bit. Uneven, not quite flat. It rests at the edge of a greater slope."

The aircraft brought us nearer the village. In the distance, the ribbon of runway came into view.

My instinct was to raise a palm and signal satisfaction with the info already given. But Denny went on, "And, finally, there is the wind. Up here it seldom moves the direction best suited for landing and takeoff."

Oh boy.

Our descent was underway. Aside from the queasy feeling brought on by the data just received, I did relish taking in the wonder of the volcanic mountain rising to meet us.

With a talent common only to seasoned bush pilots, the Frenchman brought the Cessna safely down. A smooth, glitch-free landing.

Denny's performance confirmed for me the viewpoint of a person whose opinion should count for something.

"It is possible to fly without motors, but not without knowledge and skill."

- Wilbur Wright

Chapter Thirty-Three

OASIS STREET

BUILDERS, linguists, nurses, bush pilots. . . many vocations forming the missions enterprise. High school teachers and their households, not the least.

Skirting the red, orange and purple array of bougainvillea vine, the visitor moved to Steve and Anne's veranda, and caught the sing-song welcome of her hostess, "*Kah-reee-bu!*"

Anne Street's cheery voice trilled the Swahili greeting like a free-spirited vocalist in full operetta form. The scene repeated multiple times each week as a parade of visitors dropped in. Some randomly, others by arrangement.

They came for a 'hot cuppa,' for a listening ear or a compassionate prayer. Or all the above. Often, the personal care presented by an impromptu guest carried a tangible element: needed bus fare to Kibosho or Boma Ng'ombe, school fees to cover (just this once) a high schooler about to forfeit his education because pounding hail and rain wrecked the family's maize harvest, their only viable revenue source.

This Moshi home took *wageni* (visitor) arrivals in stride. The sons, Benji, Peter and Philip, like their father — bright, industrious, mischievous —exhibited the family hospitality gene since their early days in nappies.

Anne, born and raised in Africa of British parents, grew up in farming country where her father helped manage estates for Kenya's pre-independence baron, Lord Delamere. Meeting Steve in his native England during her college years ensured that her future husband's heart would be captured — not only by her personality — but by all things Africa.

Year after year the Street's mentoring of students (elementary-age and high-schoolers alike) in the knowledge of their faith, never grew wearisome. Steve accepted a chemistry teaching spot with Moshi's international academy. His and Anne's after-school Bible Clubs came to life with spirited discussions. Wisdom was shared. And students cheered at the mention of an outing, "How about a view of Amboseli Game Park from Mount Kili?"

After some years, when the teaching position for Steve ran its course, the couple took a step back, weighed their motives and inner impressions. They drew a conclusion, "Why not?" Launching as full-time missionaries (roles they had arguably filled a long while already) came naturally. Laboring alongside their beloved pastor and friend, Wilbard.

Now, decades in, the Street's dew-drenched lawn boasted a path worn thin by flip-flops, dress shoes and bare feet. Guests of African, Asian, European, American, islander origins, and elsewhere. None kept at arm's length from Anne's infectious *"Ka-reee-bu!"*.

Home-away-from-home travelers were lodged, prayed over, teased, affirmed. Roundly blessed when the visit ended, they moved toward the screened door and out again. Beyond the bougainvillea vine.

Chapter Thirty-Four

LONDON FRIGHT

"BRANCH OUT, guys. She can't be far." *Oh Lord, Heathrow's a big place!*

The airport lay 23 kilometers west of London, a bustling swarm of 200,000 travelers any given day. I feared a sea of strangers sweeping four-year-old Amy along in some unknown direction.

Moments earlier, she stood beside me at an airport kiosk during our family's wait for a connecting flight. I paid for an item in U.S. dollars. My change came back in British sterling. In the seconds it took me to translate the coins, my daughter vanished.

Catching my urgent tone, Amy's older siblings, Julie and Scott, hurried to the stream of humanity. Patchworks of luggage trailed, emitting a low rumble throughout the terminal. My wife had fractured a toe before our Kenya departure.

From her wheelchair Ann did the one thing she could. She prayed.

Five minutes into our search, the public address system

buzzed and crackled. A voice interrupted. Male — distinctly English.

"Attention please, all passengers. May I have your attention, please? Mmm, we have with us here at Security, a young girl. She's in search of her parents. She is Amy Beth-lout."

No worry at his blending her names. Relief washed through me.

Reunited, I learned that Amy — attracted by the buzz of airport activity —stepped into the sea of travelers and simply wandered off. Discovering her isolation in the crowd minutes later, she tugged at an older man's coat.

He looked down and she asked, "Do you know my daddy?"

Following the ordeal, Ann and I regathered our emotions. Though our departure gate was nearby, the call to board would not come for a while. I called to our youngest, "Hey Angel, let's go have a donut."

Settling into a booth I surveyed her pre-kindergarten face. She lifted her milk glass. Two gulps chased a bite of pastry. Her eyebrows lifted with pleasure. A slight donut remnant shared a spot on her upper lip where a newly-fashioned milk mustache was displayed. Simple innocence.

"Amy sweetheart, Daddy needs to tell you something about airports. . . really about any places with people, you know, strangers."

I held her gaze a few seconds before the not-yet-finished donut at eye-level won out. After another bite, she looked up. Striving to be a decent parent means limping after wisdom and often finding it illusive. Fifteen years parenting children still left me feeling like a novice.

Amy sat patiently as I painted one scenario, then another — an effort to instill caution but not fear. I geared up to launch scenario-number-three about sticking close to Daddy and Mommy.

Finally, Amy sighed, "Daddy." Her tone straightforward, confiding. "Daddy, I already heard you the other times."

The drill was done, and I chuckled. Then mused somberly, *oh baby, I hope you did. I sure do.*

Chapter Thirty-Five

SHEPHERD GEMS

"FIRST THING NOW, dear, is we get that child into a harness!" The words erupted from my sister after our stateside arrival in Oklahoma City. Betty had just heard our tale of Amy's brief disappearance at the airport. It was the 1980s, the decade of Yuppies and the Dukes of Hazard — and protective child harnesses.

The alliance in the U.S. with Amy's new harness lasted her and her mom all of three weeks. We never learned where the leash ended up, perhaps a canine master's residence.

"Thanks for giving us a piece of your furlough time, for letting our teens rub shoulders with you, for telling us your Africa stories and for helping us catch a deeper vision." The green Pennsylvania hills of the church campground supplied a rich setting for the continued exchange between the pastor and us. He went on, "We're thankful, guys, for your work. Glad we get to be part of it."

Walter and Jan endeared themselves to us from the start. Their church was on the short list of our first supporting partners. Some years in we faced a dilemma. Visiting Walter's office during our next stateside visit, I inhaled deeply and rallied my courage, "The fact is, brother, our monthly support has grown pretty anemic. Your church, of course, continues giving so generously.

"Ann and I have heard a lot of messages about only trusting God to supply, that missionaries mustn't let anyone but him know their needs. What do you think, Brother Walter?"

Walter wasn't just a preacher. He was a friend, a pastor's pastor, the kind that majored on listening. In the currency of Walter's vocabulary, he didn't trade in pat answers. He wasn't one to dish out clichés.

Leveling a sympathetic gaze, he spoke after a brief pause, "The way I see it, brother, every mission work has money needs, family support needs, work project needs. Here's the thing: there are plenty of folks in God's family with resources to invest, and they're happy to do it. The only problem is, where they don't know there is a need, they can't easily come alongside. People need information. They need to know. Yours is the voice to inform them.

"Sharing with God's family is a gift you're offering them, an opportunity to invest in things that matter. Not just now, but forever. Then the issue is off your shoulders. God speaks to the ones he chooses, and they respond as they feel. It's not on you. Pass on the vision, brother. Let God supply."

By our next stateside visit, the mission ledger was displaying a healthier report.

"...So that having all sufficiency in all things at all times, you may abound in every good work." - Second Corinthians 9:8 (ESV)

Chapter Thirty-Six

LOUD AND CLEAR

A MISSION PASTOR once asked my wife to preach for an upcoming Sunday service. But *only* once.

William Moseti, a man of little schooling, displayed qualities people admire in a leader. Kindness, humility, wisdom — a warm-hearted chuckle behind a ready smile. Pastor Moseti had assigned our firstborn child a nickname.

Two-year-old Julie, abounding in energy, woke up each morning with a zest for life. In her often-excited moments, she could get loud. For Pastor William, the label for Julie, *"Duka-la-kelele"* (the noise store) fit perfectly.

"Mama Julie," Pastor William greeted Ann as they crossed paths on the mission station. "You must give the sermon this Sunday."

Most people can note a time when a perfect response is called for.

"Sure, Pastor," Ann smiled. "I'll be glad to, but only if you will watch *Duka-la-kelele* for me while I speak."

When service time came, William happily took his preaching spot at the mission pulpit.

Tending to the cares of little ones under their charge, young mothers across the globe rival the world's strongest endurance athletes. Ann made do with rationed bathing water during dry seasons while attending to her cloth-diapered babies. She also rushed to the aid of each child whenever a crisis broke out.

- when toddler Scott was run over by a motorcycle steered by a biker-wannabe —her teenaged boyfriend the self-appointed driving coach.
- when five-year-old Amy careened face-first to the gravelly playground off a towering sliding board's highest perch —her poor face battered and momentarily rearranged.
- through a long night vigil at Julie's bedside during an especially painful ear infection.

Our family's bouts with everything from food poisoning to parasites to malaria and any number of added afflictions were regularly met with Ann's prompt, skilled, and prayerful action. A pithy verse from a collection of poetry beckons a response her family members gratefully offer,

"Honor her for all that her hands have done, and let her works bring her praise at the city gate." - Proverbs 31.31 (NIV)

Chapter Thirty-Seven

A MANY SPLENDORED THING

"Do you take this woman to be your wedded wife?

What steps across this great earth lead a man and woman to so pledge their lives, "I take this person to be. . ."?

Life outside the U.S. had been stretching my thinking. Musings stirred about cultural traditions, of courtship, of marriage —some fun and romance-laden, others not, but interesting all the same.

"Well, you know," offered the Asian gent whose head often wagged sideways in agreement, "It's like this. . . ."

I nodded to my Indian friend, coaxing him on as steam from hot chai waltzed about our cup rims.

"You know, we in India and other places come to marriage differently than you in the West. And, though modern times bring some change, customs to do with the marital union — we hold them quite dear."

Interesting.

"Can I ask you, Vinay, did your grandparents decide how your mother and father were to meet and marry? Your father's parents, for instance, did they select who the girl would be for him?"

Ahead of my chat with Vinay, I had already been hearing how most of the world did romance and marriage in ways I thought weird. Like everyone else, I interpreted most things through my personal, cultural lens.

"They played a big role, yes," Vinay replied. "And, so did my mother's family with long visits over tea and step-by-step discussions continuing right up to the ceremony.

"After all, marrying is not about falling in love."

My cup halted partway to my lips.

"It is about giving thought to *life*, which usually does, of course, include marrying someone. "

I nodded, implying I understood. Vinay seemed to take it for granted that I actually did.

"Young people in the West follow feelings. They go with their senses. A couple falls in love and they marry.

"In our tradition we find it better to wed a person the family determines, in their best judgment, to be a decent match. The process moves forward. Eventually, the couple marry. The two then grow into loving one another. . . Yes, it usually comes. The pair grow to love each other over time. It is the way with our people."

These worlds of romance, courtship and marriage. West and East. Could there be a middle ground?

Long before I met her, my own future-bride had nearly drowned. She was young at the time, mere hours old.

Chapter Thirty-Eight

BRIDE BARGAIN

"MR. AND MRS. BARNES, the risks are high. To our knowledge no baby has made it through long-term. But the surgery is the only chance your little girl has."

Earl and Mary had little time to think it over. A surgical team gathered, and a T. E. Fistula repair was scheduled. The life of Alice Ann Barnes — her full body weight shy of five pounds — hung in the balance.

T.E. stood for Tracheosophageal. Sadly, the baby's esophagus and trachea were defective at birth. Designed to transport her mother's milk into her stomach, Ann's esophagus mingled with her air-tube. Thus, any nutrition-rich fluids were sent to her lungs, not her stomach. In 1949 the field of medicine had its limits. Without corrective surgery, death by drowning or malnutrition would likely result.

Anesthetics were administered, their effects carefully watched. The surgeon's knife found entrance into little Ann's back. The procedure was underway.

Hours passed as anxious parents waited.

"Her vitals are steady." Intensive care nurses — hours into

post-op —kept a close watch on little Ann. Some likely prayed.

December 1967. The former pediatrics patient — poised, lovely in her white gown — strode down the sanctuary's center aisle toward her waiting groom.

Our courtship, Ann's and mine, had largely played out by long distance, spanning twelve hundred miles and two-and-a-half years. First by old-fashioned letters. Then with my Oklahoma-to-Montana phone calls.

The marriage wasn't arranged by third-party players, but neither did we magically fall in love. We grew toward one another through the modest media of stationery paper and ballpoint ink, radial-dial phones with long-distance lines transporting two distinctly different accents — one from just south of Canada, the other a stone's throw from Texas.

We had survived, each of us, our childhood crises of health. To one day embark, united, on a journey unlike any we could have dreamed.

An arranged marriage, one might say. By providence.

◊◊◊

"Thirty-eight," the young man replied.

"Really? Thirty-eight?"

My new friend's voice was matter-of-fact. "Thirty-eight cows."

How does an Oklahoma boy digest rural Africa's matrimony language?

"But suppose the young man can't come up with that many? What happens?"

"Oh, sometimes the girl's father negotiates. . . you know, back and forth."

"And if they still can't agree on a number that works?"

"Well, the young man goes away, with hopes the *mzee* will somehow lower the dowry. The girl's father also hopes. . . that a more well-off suitor comes by."

◊◊◊

What's the delay?

I had grown impatient this past half hour. It was wedding day. I had been volunteered to drive the bride and attendants from her family home — a simple dwelling well off the beaten path — to the church. A decked-out choral group waited, watching for our arrival. The groom likewise waited. And waited.

"Brother Jerry, it seems the old man wants more cows or more money. . . or something. . . an added dowry, a sum not discussed earlier, to close the arrangement."

As the fussing went on, the bridegroom's rep labored to persuade the old man. A diesel-smoke-belching two-ton lorry entered the grounds. Twenty adults, mostly women in colorful dress, several men formally garmented jostled about within trying to stay upright as the truck half-circled to a stop.

Because of the last-minute dowry challenge the festive mood had subsided. All appeared resigned to wait things out. Apparently, the tactical game wasn't so new to the tribe. They got the picture. *Give the old man time. He likely won't risk losing face before the clan leaders by sticking in his heels much longer. Not for adding a mere one or two more skinny cows.*

My curiosity grew. *How would this turn out?*

I waited in the car while the bride-to-be and her attendants did what females do in an African wedding prep-hut. Excited giggles floated past thin walls to the outside.

Turning my attention again to where the feisty papa of the

bride had parked himself, I noticed what appeared to be an attitude shift. The gray-haired man, in his effort to extract more dowry treasures from the groom's family, raised his hand slowly. The patriarch tilted his head downward and nodded — signaling, I hoped, a civil concession.

Glancing to the east, I winced. *Those gathering clouds headed our way.*

An outbreak of measured laughter sounded from the gathering of elders near the old man. Then excited jostling and laughter as the open lorry took in more eager passengers. All was good. Car doors swung open. The bride and three of her maids squished themselves with their bright billowing dresses into my vehicle.

Due to the drawn-out dowry bargaining, the ceremony started late. It was rainy season, and the early afternoon downpour pounded the church's tin roof. The volume rose, all but muting the voices of the bride and groom pledging their mutual devotion.

African weddings. Nothing quite like them. I smiled. Drenched celebrants — including those trying with colorful umbrellas to stave off the blowing torrent — hooted, sang and celebrated.

The deluge finally passed. Despite the wet conditions and the dowry drama, the knot was tied. All was well.

Festivities drawn to a close, the Peugeot with her wet and weary navigator at the wheel, sloshed and slid along muddy rivulets to the main road.

Reentering our home six hours later, I gratefully received the mug of hot chai *my* bride offered me at the door. Moving toward a room where dry garments awaited, I chuckled back to her, "Even at 38 cows, darlin', you would have been a great bargain!"

Chapter Thirty-Nine

A BEWILDERING

CONSIDERING the severe hardships missionaries have encountered through the centuries, our valley of 1984 could seem trite by comparison. For us it was raw pain.

What just happened?

The question sent us reeling as my wife and I made our way back from Dallas to our temporary residence in East Texas — Carthage. Our family was part way through a stateside furlough.

Ann and I had served in East Africa for 12 years. We had just been broadsided by news that we may be disinvited to return to our post. The past six years had been among the richest of our lives. Amy, our cheery third-born, was added to our family a year ago. Her siblings, Julie and Scott, were content as ever — growing friendships, learning, thriving. The extension training I developed in the region had expanded and, by every account, was well received by those it served.

"You need to fly to Nairobi, Jerry. I think it's necessary for you to clear the air with what's going on with you and the Kenyan leadership."

The senior-most American leader in the Africa work offered his advice in a matter-of-fact voice. Yet, his manner conveyed an ominous urgency. "You need to meet with the Council face-to-face to get this resolved."

We left the Dallas restaurant having barely touched our salads, both of us bewildered. After a few silent miles, Ann spoke. "What was that *about*. . . Get *what* resolved, Jerry?" Ann's words echoed my own upside-down ponderings. *What is happening. . . what?*

As the bombshell news seeped its way into our souls, Ann and I were reminded of a hint of something a few days earlier. A co-worker and friend had phoned us from Kenya, feeling compelled to connect. He shared about some fuzzy word going around that missionary Lout was possibly in trouble. But no details accompanied the reports. All he heard were guesses, conjectures. No one defined what seemed to be afoot.

Saint John of the Cross spoke of "the dark night of the soul."

The dark had started descending. Soon I would board a plane to cross the world, not knowing why.

◊◊◊

"God whispers to us in our pleasures, speaks in our conscience, but shouts in our pain: it is His megaphone to rouse a deaf world."

   - C.S. Lewis, *The Problem of Pain*

What awaits me down there?

A few minutes earlier, as the great aircraft began its

descent to Nairobi's mile-high runway, I had drawn the Navy-blue passenger blanket away from my head and shoulders. The covering had served to conceal a stubborn trickle of tears.

I had not come to this place entirely on my own. God journeyed together with Ann and me from the outset. Even along this sudden bewildering trail, a pathway ending who knew where. Still, I could not recall ever bearing such a sense of aloneness.

I sat in a cloister of fellow passengers gazing out the plane's window onto a land beneath, of fifteen million inhabitants. It didn't matter. Alone is alone regardless the surroundings.

Lord, I do need your presence. Be near me these coming days.

My tired mind rehearsed the sequence of happenings these past weeks.

What was the missing piece, the accusation, the scandal? Was there one? Why would I be disinvited to serve in this land, among this people we had grown to care deeply for?

The grand ball of sun had for an hour been inching its way above the Indian Ocean 300 miles eastward. Its revealing light stretched inland, drenching the Nairobi Game Park that lay near the capital city's airport. Giraffe, zebra, antelope and the occasional pride of lion had long wakened to the sun's encroaching blaze, their animal senses already on high alert. Even as I detected my own protective instincts rising.

As with all long-term residents coming from an outside culture, I had made my share of goofs: mispronounced language, klutzy embarrassments that locals regularly let slide. In the end though, search for it as I might, no complaint of violating any cultural, moral or religious codes came to mind.

Thuh-THUMP. The plane touched down. Her sturdy tires moved toward the mobile stairways.

I was "home," where I had first landed a dozen years ago. But this landing was different, the first time in my overseas travels without my dear wife. She and our children, thousands of miles distant, awaited word of my safe arrival. I felt the sense of aloneness again threaten.

Mercifully, a flight attendant's voice, "Please take care leaving, ladies and gentlemen. Remember your carry-on items. And mind the steps as you move down to the tarmac."

Chapter Forty

PUZZLEMENT AND PROMISE

STEPPING OUTSIDE, I paused atop the mobile platform and drew in the African air. As I trailed a chatty group of tourists downward toward the tarmac, I stole a further look across the Kenyan landscape.

How much longer will this be our home?

A line of counsel shared a dozen years earlier revisited, "When you get out there and when things get really hard—remember this. . . ."

The words had hung above the table between us.

My mentor, veteran missionary Johansson, had leaned forward in his chair, apparently for emphasis. It was early 1972 near Rochester, New York, a few days before Ann and I would fly to Africa, embarking on the adventure of our lives. I probably wasn't ready for his three-word punchline.

"Remember," he emphasized, "when things get really hard. Love your wife."

Now a dozen years later, I was poised to open a conference room door in Nairobi and face the distressing thing awaiting me.

Remember. Love your wife.

Before we entered our own trial, I had heard of married couples so undone by hardships and testings, the best they could muster at the end of a day was to silently weep themselves to sleep in each other's arms. Ann and I had entered this level of broken.

Yet, a curious thing had also been happening. In the tunnel of conflicted voices and questionings, I sensed a quiet invitation. To the Psalms, the ancient song book at the Bible's center. The readings became my home, my refuge. I blubbered its lyrics, reviewed its whimperings and its railings, poured over it from my soul. And comfort came out of hiding, to find me.

We drew from the Psalms together, Ann and me. Even now, with seas and continents between.

I entered the room where the Kenyan leaders awaited. Senior overseers offered handshakes. Courtesy marked their faces. A measure of warmth blended with a measure of awkwardness.

Are these men feeling as mystified as me?

The meeting commenced.

Two hours later, the visit was over, and I left almost as puzzled as before. But, in an odd way, I was comforted. And greatly relieved. A question had surfaced among the men. Some voiced it several times.

"Why is our brother here? Why the cost, the long flights?"

Closing comments wrapped up the time.

"Brother Jerry," the senior spokesman's words came quiet, sincere. "Whatever difficulties there may have been in your service with us, there is nothing we see that should call for you to make this big and costly trip. We really do not understand. Please give our greetings to your wife. We look forward to receiving you back to the work when your time in America is done."

Before I reached the airport for my return flight home, a signed letter from the Council was passed to me. Offering well-wishes and words of "Sorry" for undue pain brought our way. The message kindly addressed Ann by name and affirmed the African leadership's readiness that we continue in the work.

The aircraft started its lumbered movement toward an outbound runway. "Ladies and gentlemen, we are preparing for take-off. Please see that your carry-on items are safely secured. . . ."

Drawing my seat belt about me I took in a slow breath. *Lord, you surely have things for us to learn. Don't let your counsel be lost to us.*

A treasured piece of literature lay open before me, precious phrases strung together I could easily recite from young childhood.

"He leads me in paths of righteousness for his name's sake." From the Psalms.

Chapter Forty-One

PIVOTAL STANDOFF

"I GO to the Coast to mock him. And to beat him when he shows the lie!"

The big man was strong, menacing. Anyone having experience with Alexander Aidini knew his threat was not small talk.

"He is no man of God, this foreigner!" the angry African spat out. "He comes to our land a trickster. Come. . . we shall beat him together. . . all of us. We go to Mombasa!"

The target of Aidini's contempt was an American preacher.

T. L. Osborn had traveled with his evangelistic team from Oklahoma to Kenya's coastal city on the Indian Ocean. "To preach the gospel, to proclaim Jesus Christ in power, to heal and deliver and bring salvation."

Osborn's multiple preaching campaigns were known to draw thousands, with large numbers of the sick and suffering. Aidini was sure all was a hoax to exploit the masses. He would show it up for what it was.

Among the half dozen toughs accompanying Aidini was a man whose mother was blind.

"Bring your mother with us, bring Mama *Zaila*. When the white man makes prayer for healing in the meeting, we will put her there. When her eyes remain dark and she is not well, this will show the lie. And there we will move, we will break the *mzungu (white man)* just there!" Five days travel brought them to their destination.

Leaving their Land Rover beneath a gnarled tree, the group entered the massive stream of tribal people. They continued by foot toward the blaring loudspeaker. Mombasa's port-city atmosphere with its salty aroma felt heavy, humid.

"Take care, Mama Zaila, do not rush. Hold tight to my arm." The woman clung to her son, her useless eyes staring into blackness.

Africa is a vast continent with pockets of dense populations swarming across sprawling cities. Still, the crowd flooding Mombasa's big outdoor field, was bigger than any the Congolese visitors had known. It was clear the name Osborn evoked interest.

The half-dozen strangers from a thousand miles westward pushed their way deeper into the crowd, their goal the big wooden stage where the *mzungu preacher* and his wife, Daisy sat. At either side of the American couple were local dignitaries, invited along with several African church and mission heads.

Poised before the stage, the Congolese gang awaited their moment. For Aidini, it could not come soon enough.

Preacher Osborn's voice rang strong, echoing across the mass of gathered humanity. The deceitfulness of sin, its destructive fruit in a life. Then of the power of forgiveness, of the cross of Jesus, of hope in him.

The evangelist paused, then turned to a different emphasis. "Do we have anyone troubled in their body tonight?"

As the air hung quiet above the throng, heads began to nod. Calls of *"Ndiyo" (yes)* sounded from the Mombasa crowd.

"If you are lame, cannot move about well or cannot see. . . if your body has stopped working in some way. And if you believe Jesus came to free you, to heal you both soul and body, this is your time to believe him. Do we believe Jesus?"

A ringing chorus rose, "Yes!"

"Well, now we're going to pray. Remember it is Jesus who heals. I cannot heal anyone. Jesus. He is the deliverer. As the book of Hebrews tells us, *'Jesus is the same yesterday and today and forever!'* Tell me now, is he the same for *your* life? Can you trust his love, trust his power? Believe him! He wants you well."

The evangelist with the soft Oklahoma drawl held firmly to his mic. His voice passionate, marked with sincerity. "Now, let me pray with you. The resurrected Jesus is here. And he will heal. . . will deliver in these moments just now."

T. L. Osborn prayed. The words simple, clear, strong, with evident conviction. Not a lengthy prayer.

"Now friends, if anyone brought a deaf friend here today, you check with that friend. Look them in the face. Ask them, can you hear?"

As the minister went on with prayer, brief words of guidance and of referencing the Bible, a shout erupted a few feet from where he stood, "Ayeee, Ayeee!"

The shouting voice was Zaila's. She had willed her eyes open the moment the preacher had called out a phrase, "In Jesus' name, be healed!"

A momentary lull followed, then. . . "Ayeee, Ayeee, Ayeee!"

Wide-eyed with vision, Zaila's shout of triumph startled Alexander Aidini who stood inches away. Her outburst continued. "I see! I see! . . . I see your face, Mzee Aidini! I see you, I see!"

Aidini had tasted little personal fear over the years. He often brought fear to others. Fear had not come his way. But now.

Alexander's inner self trembled. The big man quaked, coming undone in the presence of a force unlike anything he had known.

A shouting, crying Zaila went on, caught up in astonished delight. "Mzee! Mzee Aidini! Nakuona (I am seeing you)! Mzee, hii ni Yesu! (It is Jesus. Jesus!)"

At last, Aidini, overcome by conviction, drew himself together. He found his voice. "I want to get saved. Tell me. How do I get saved?"

Chapter Forty-Two

LIGHT THE MATCH

Spirits. Good. Evil.

What is this thing, this world of spirits? How real is the unseen world? Do invisible personalities carry influence, power with people — sometimes over them?

I often pondered the questions. Growing up in the Pentecostal faith, I heard the spirit-world referenced plenty of times: demon-oppression, spiritual warfare, deliverance ministry. My understanding was limited but the world of spirits seemed reasonably obvious.

Teachers of scripture and the Bible itself shone light on the subject. Though God himself is supreme, having no rival, no equal, much of humanity suffers in some measure under the deceiver, the accuser. This view, with plenty of Bible to commend the topic, informed much of my belief about spirit beings.

For me, it was also personal. I had at times – especially in my youth – sensed a thing that felt like a dark, eerie presence. Not often but enough to trouble me, leaving me unsettled and sometimes fearful.

Living now in deep Africa, I discovered something I had long heard. *The world at large — outside North American, European and other Western cultures — needed no persuading whether the spirit world existed. They required no convincing if spirit beings played a role in living, breathing human beings.*

First-hand encounters with witchcraft jarred me out of any guesswork about the matter.

———

"Yeah, that'd be great! I'll check with Ann." Catching up over lunch with missionary friends, Jerry and Sharon, would foster updates, fresh stories, laughter.

Jerry taught in a vocational school. The tribal people of the region had generations-long histories featuring spiritual powers they knew to be evil. Placing curses on adversaries was as common in some areas as the presence of moisture was common to the rainy season. Divination, witchcraft and the like saw powerful spiritual influences, fueled by fear.

"Mister Jerry, Mister Jerry!"

The youth on the bike sped toward us from the school's direction a mile away.

My friend set his tea cup down and walked outside.

After a brief exchange with the boy, Jerry called up, "A student at the school is in trouble. Want to come with me?"

We set off on the ragged road, hardly more than a foot path. Less than five minutes later, the car jostled to a stop.

A tall, robust-looking youth sat on an outcropping of rock common to the area. The student looked like a fine specimen of health. Except for his demeanor. And the trembling hands. His eyes shifted repeatedly away from direct contact. They seemed dark, fearful. He held his head as in a vice, sandwiched in a tight grip between the palms of his large hands.

My friend gently questioned the boy and a pair of his friends. The boy suffered an overpowering head-throb. It pulsed with searing pain. Indeed, he looked tortured.

But the pain's source was not biological. Not really.

"Somebody from his home village sent it to him. Someone with a grudge. The envelope with that stuff inside came hand-delivered yesterday and he's been like this since."

What led up to this moment? Curse updates don't often happen in my native Oklahoma hills. But this thing seemed really serious.

Summoning the unusual parcel, the missionary noticed the opened envelope bulged a bit. In it was a strange assortment. Random, spooky things not commonly fit for having around.

"Elements of a curse. Whoever sent it to Omondi wasn't playing games. They planned real physical and mental harm. Even death. Look at these bone fragments, the ashes mixed in, these bits of rock."

We eyed the elements warily. Something became clear. The recipient of this "gift," *knew* he had been cursed. His fear was real. Omondi knew he could die at the hand of the power behind these items. Invisible but real, a terribly dark force too strong to withstand.

Jerry and I stood silently, each in our own thoughts. Both of us anxious. Each of us sensed the other was praying, groping for guidance. How do you contend with this kind of thing? In another setting one could shrug it off as a game of foolish superstition. But we sensed this to be a full-on display of an evil presence, dispatched somehow to render harm. What could we do?

A thought began to stir. Pushing past a temptation to ignore it, I turned to my friend.

"Jerry, would you mind if we try something?" He waited

for me to go on. "Can someone bring matches? I think we need to urge this young man to resist, that he fights this thing in the power of Christ."

Only partly-sure of my instinct, I continued. My confidence grew.

"I believe he needs to break this curse and we can be there with him. We can pray. But I think he needs to set these things on fire and destroy them. It will be his statement of God's claim on his life. If he's willing to, that is."

Jerry nodded.

As I spoke the words, I knew I was out of my depth. I trembled on the inside as much as Omondi on the outside.

Matches were brought. We moved to an enclosure and sat on the floor, Jerry and I at either side of Omondi.

After sharing Scripture, we affirmed the goodness and the truth of Jesus and the power of his name. We asked Omondi if he agreed with Jesus's words. "Do you believe God has power above all?"

He nodded slightly and we pressed ahead, inviting him to offer himself fully to Jesus Christ. Slowly, deliberately he voiced a prayer of surrender to God. Jerry and I never let up calling on the Lord from our hearts.

After a moment I looked into the young man's eyes.

"Good. Now Omondi, do you renounce all witchcraft of any kind? Do you reject all spirit forces that oppose the Lord Jesus? Can you say that you do?"

Weakly, he whispered, "Yes." When asked one more time, he came back with an assertive, "Yes."

I raised the envelope with its contents. Some apprehension seemed to play at his eyes. But his fear had lessened. Jerry and I sensed Omondi was choosing freedom. We kept praying, "Help him, Lord Jesus. Be near."

"Alright now, let's light the match."

His hand trembled with such intensity, I took his hand in mine. We gripped the match together. Thankful for his clear resolve to continue, we struck the match and lit the envelope and contents. Jerry and I voiced thanksgivings to Jesus the whole time. And a beautiful thing followed.

Witnessing the flame take over the elements, we felt a release of joy. The three of us came to our feet. Jerry and I called out in joy and conviction, praising the name of our Lord. Fear had left. Had left us all. Omondi's head pain went away. Deliverance had come.

As we prepared to leave, the name of a pastor I knew from Omondi's home area came to mind. I sent a message to him. The two connected several days later.

At the end of the day we were at peace. Wow!

The power of Christ prevailed over raw evil. And two young less-than-fearless missionaries had been invited to take part.

No wonder it's called Good News.

We had witnessed the authority of Christ's name. A power greater than witchcraft, greater than fear. Even death. The power of love. . . cause for deep-hearted praise.

Chapter Forty-Three

UNASSUMING GIANTS

UNNERVING. Getting interrupted while giving a public talk, especially when demons are involved.

Through our Kenya and Tanzania years I grew thankful for the wisdom and courage of African servants of Jesus. Many challenged me in positive ways — not by direct words, but by life-example — in discernment and spiritual authority.

How do you counsel the second wife of a polygamous, unbelieving husband, who has come to faith in Christ?

Such tricky problems are not easily fixed through pat answers by well-meaning outsiders. Simple solutions do not fare well in the world of the complex. Cultural divides compound the matter. Reconciling family traditions to the Way of Jesus demands patience, grace and wisdom.

What a relief to discover I served among church leaders who understood how to rightly address baffling questions that I and my fellow expats were clueless about.

"There are two equal and opposite errors into which our race can fall about the devils. One is to disbelieve in their existence. The

other is to believe, and to feel an excessive and unhealthy interest in them." Few people can distill a truth better than C.S. Lewis.

Why the screaming?

The lake region seemed a magnet for demons. Generations of witchcraft flung regional doors open to dark displays of the invisible underworld.

Taking my place behind a simple wooden pulpit, I rested my Bible and surveyed the gathering. A lake breeze made its way inland, blunting the oppressive mid-day heat. It was District Convention time and congregations from the area had set up makeshift shelters of straw to shield from the sun's brutal rays. Three days of teaching, of celebrating, of praying and of feasting were underway.

I had barely begun my message when a troubled woman rose in the audience. Her first cries were moderate. But quickly became louder. A rhythmic chant followed, growing shriller, more distressing by the moment. Soon she seemed out of control or under the control of an alien influence.

Without my uttering a word or signaling for any help, two tribal gentlemen moved quickly to the woman's side. Addressing her in moderate but deliberate tones, the men succeeded in relocating her to a space a short distance from our gathering.

Later I learned these men had experience in exorcising bad spirits from the demonically-troubled.

My audience seemed unrattled by the interruption and I resumed preaching. Several minutes of my early remarks from scripture were only slightly muffled by shouts from the deliverance quarters, "Come out of her. Out in Jesus's name!"

All the while the poor woman's unnatural voice ebbed and flowed with irregular volume. At last all went silent. The freed lady re-entered the meeting and conducted herself in a perfectly civil manner.

I thanked God these wise, Holy Spirit-empowered Africans – unassuming giants – answered the call to challenges beyond our pay grade. Teaching me by example that the useful missionary does well to observe. Learners.

Thank you, Lord. And help us.

◊◊◊

When noting the kinds of things God does through ordinary people, philosopher Dallas Willard would fondly cite the term "divine conspiracy".

"The world can no longer be left to mere diplomats, politicians, and business leaders. They have done the best they could, no doubt. But this is an age for spiritual heroes - a time for men and women to be heroic in their faith and in spiritual character and power."

Chapter Forty-Four

TAVERN MAKOVER

As a child, the term Belgian Congo would never have crossed my mind separate from images of Tarzan trapezing lofty vines, crying his trademark jungle yodel. Nor would I have seen myself ever addressing a crowd in that place deep in the heart of Africa.

Especially at one place.

Moving to the pulpit of the capital city's downtown church, I was greeted by the pastor, a man I heard was a former anti-Christian militant. Alexander Aidini.

The throng of Congolese worshippers acknowledged me — their out-of-country guest —with happy shouts of welcome. My friend, Ben Dodzweit, introduced me in their native Lingala.

Pastor Aidini's journey from Gospel foe to disciple-of-Jesus was by now thirty years in the making. The accounts of his pilgrimage left me nothing less than awed.

Not long after his dramatic conversion in Mombasa, Aidini answered a call to Christian service. Art Dodzweit, Ben's uncle, had taken the rough-around-the-edges disciple into his mentoring care. Following a stint in Uganda, Aidini returned to his Congo home and its capital, Kinshasa. In time forces opposed to colonial rule overthrew the Congo and assigned it the name *Zaire*.

Along the way, Aidini's fiery devotion to Jesus grew. And unusual things followed.

A police officer's wife had fallen ill. Aidini was summoned to pray over her. No results.

"Bring your witchcraft charms and symbols," the preacher challenged the woman. "Burn them in Jesus' name! Turn from these dark things and receive God's freedom."

She agreed. With the sorcery items destroyed, more prayer followed. The woman recovered.

Claiming a preaching spot near a traffic round-about the evangelist showed up at four p.m. each day.

Little seemed to come of the meetings until one day Mary, a deranged woman passed by naked. Within earshot of his preaching. Aidini directed his words to her, rebuking evil spirits tormenting the woman. A calm came over her. Ladies came forward with garments and covered her.

Brought to freedom from that day, the joyful woman testified often at Aidini's round-about gathering. Many people of the neighborhood, long aware of her miserable past, came to listen. New believers were added.

"I will play you my machine," he shouted, hoisting an old typewriter over his head.

This second possessed person, a bare-bottomed man named Ronald, happened by Evangelist Aidini's location. Evil spirits were called out. His vigorous testimony spoke of wandering the city streets tormented, ever parading the beat-up type-writer. Finally, he was freed at the roadway intersection. Week by week the crowd swelled, eventually numbering hundreds.

With the help of sympathetic followers, the preacher rented the *Congo Bar* on Sunday mornings. But area prostitutes began losing business as more people converted.

A municipal governor was summoned to confront Aidini. "You must stop your meetings in the bar."

The preacher turned to the official. His reply came with a boldness the onlookers had grown accustomed to.

"In three days, you, sir, will no longer be governor." Before the time period passed, a random circumstance forced the official to vacate his post.

As the work expanded, funds came available through a visiting Swiss man, stirred by things he had witnessed. Soon the gathered band of believers took ownership of the long-standing beer joint.

As a tribute to the transforming nature of the gospel, the place was renamed *Congo Bar Church.*

My preaching visit to Congo Bar in 1986 came about through a yearning. Not a hunger to preach in a large city church but a stirring in my wife and me. To launch from Kenya, go elsewhere in Africa, and begin serving there. Given the continent was home to more than fifty countries — which one?

"In their hearts humans plan their course, but the Lord establishes their steps." - Proverbs 16:9 (NIV)

◊◊◊

From a disarming "So you're the man with the black heart," Ann and I had grown fond of Carlton Spencer. The early connection with the ministry statesman factored into our maiden assignment to East Africa. Now, finding ourselves at another missions crossroads, his remarks carried a hint of *déjà vu*.

Elim Chairman Spencer stood relaxed before a company of missionaries at our annual general meeting outside Nairobi. "Several of you have served in this beautiful land for some years. I sense the Lord's nudge, that some of you may find a stirring within. A stir to one day pass beyond Kenya's borders, on to other fields less-visited by our Lord's good message."

Both of us, my Ann and I, felt a stir. Following soul-searchings and times in prayer, our conviction grew that we were to venture to a new field.

"We know the mission serves regions westward," I mused. "And to the south as well."

So, I flew the fifteen hundred miles to Kinshasa and found myself before a crowd in a renovated bar.

Aidini's ministry had dramatically multiplied the past three decades. Church congregations now numbered more than 3,000 across Zaire's enormous landscape. The leadership-training workforce needed more people.

After two weeks poising as best I could the spiritual antenna of my heart, I boarded my Nairobi flight home with no new sense of clarity. None.

We turned our attention to Kenya's big neighbor to the south, the land of famed explorer-missionary, Doctor David Livingstone. This time I would not go alone. We crossed into Tanzania at the Namanga border.

What surprise lay ahead.

Chapter Forty-Five

NOTABLE MARKERS

"I KEEP RETURNING TO IT, hon, this scripture verse." Ann leafed to the center of her Bible. "This Psalm.

"'I will instruct you and teach you in the way which you shall go, I will guide you with my eye,' Psalm 32:8. The words keep coming back to mind." Taking Ann's experience to heart, the promise reinforced our faith.

Days later, passing through Namanga Village with minimal drama, I slid into the Peugeot driver's seat. As I handed our freshly-stamped U.S. passports to Ann, I engaged the clutch and nudged the gear lever forward. Turning to my bride of nearly twenty years, I grinned, "Well, here's a first for me, sweetheart. I've never driven Tanzania's roads."

Tonight, we would lodge at the home of friends whose surname — considering their missionary vocation — brought a smile. . . the Angels.

Granger and Beverly Angel's Arusha home sat a short distance from Tengeru Village and the church they had pioneered. They now co-led with Tanzanian Pastor Charles Nkya.

As we breezed southward along the paved highway, taking in the ever-enlarging image of fourteen-thousand-foot Mount Meru, I silently reviewed bits of a sermon-in-the-making. Tomorrow's Sunday service would find me at the Tengeru Church pulpit.

With scripture and illustrations, encouragements and challenges, the next morning I wrapped up the sermon, inviting believers to further yield their lives to God's oversight and care. As sermons go, I was pleased, thankful for his presence and aware nothing noteworthy seemed afoot — at least to my knowledge. The service dismissed. Several folks lingered.

Up walked Zahira, a lady Elder in the church.

Zahira, small but poised, taught in a local college. She carried herself with quiet grace. When she had first opened her life to Christ and stepped away from the family religion, her Muslim husband threw her and her infant from the home. Keeping the older children to himself, he forbade Mama Zahira to visit them.

Through deep pain, she pressed ahead in love and zeal for her Savior, growing a keen devotion through the years. In the companionship of fellow believers, she found a deepening strength in Scripture reading and prayer.

Zahira's Bible lay open in her hand as she approached Pastor Angel. Placing her free palm to the page she signaled a passage. "Pastor, this verse — I feel God has this scripture for our guests from Kenya. Can you share it with them?"

Granger responded with a smile, "No, Zahira. The Lord has given this to you. *You* just go over to them and share it."

Moving our direction, her finger still resting on the text, Mama Zahira quietly cleared her throat. "Brother and Sister, I feel God has this verse for you. It came to me during the preaching today."

I noted the reference and took in the Swahili words. Pausing a moment, I turned to Ann and, with a chuckle, asked pointedly, "Does this resonate in any way?"

Her face lit up as the text came into focus,

"I will instruct you and teach you in the way which you shall go, I will guide you with my eye."

Chapter Forty-Six

A PLACE TO TURN

FEW AFRICANS NEED CONVINCING that the spirit world lives and thrives. Regularly running head-long into curse-induced afflictions and other displays of dark powers, thousands across the continent have broken the spell. Radical deliverance comes to them through faith in Christ, their healer.

A friend and I had joined up with Jesus and renounced a spirit by invoking the Lord's name. We watched a man get freed from fear, perhaps escaping death.

A thrill follows, euphoria even. But then a distressing memory from our own life visits the mind. Troubling questions follow.

What of my own demons?

I had met Christ in my youth. God's good presence flooded over and through me, wave on wave. The first occasion came at my "Yes" to a simple invitation, voiced by a lay-pastor, "Would you like more of Jesus?"

God had kept me from the prison of an iron lung and brought my polio-ravaged limbs to life. His Spirit then chased after me and my rebellious teen heart. That encounter melted me to brokenness and restored me to family.

Then, wonder of wonders, he brought to me my most prized treasure, an inside/outside beauty from the Big Sky state of Montana.

Yet. My secret held on. And its attending darkness.

The night Lawrence violated me in my pre-puberty childhood set the stage for compounded issues fueled by shame. Through wrongful, impure ways, Lawrence exposed me to sexuality. This trauma set in motion desires I knew to be wrong. Repeated cycles of guilt-inducing thoughts and behaviors followed. Behaviors I yearned to be freed of plagued me regardless my efforts to resist.

And try I did.

While on the one hand my life was marked by blessings too good to be true, I struggled deeply with periodic bouts of distress over crippling addictions.

Crippled. A missionary with a limp.

Struggles and questionings aside, the call to serve helped anchor me. I believed the Lord had work for me to do so I pressed ahead, knowing he loved me, that he was after my best. Even as I wrestled with a sense of unworthiness and the occasional feeling I was a junky heap of damaged goods, the assurance of his care sustained me. I knew who deserved credit. Not me, that was certain.

When some useful cause might arise: sponsoring a student, leading a class, encouraging a co-laborer of my own culture or another I felt at home. The discordant clamorings of unhealthy desire quieted. I poured out my energies, my prayers for others.

"The sacrifices of God are a broken spirit; a broken and contrite heart, O God, you will not despise."

The ancient passage consoled me again and again through

my bitter-sweet years. Laying my wounded heart before him was all I knew to do. Turning myself over to his mercy, repeatedly, sincerely.

"All that the Father gives me shall come to me; and he that comes to me I will in no wise cast out."

Rehearsing such verses before him tethered me. His mercy remained a constant. Ever meeting me in my places of brokenness, never condemning while never at the same time giving me a pass.

Regret — shame — contrition — repentance — thanksgiving. The cycles continued, ending every time at the door of mercy from one nearer than a brother. Jesus. Friend of sinners.

My theme verse may well have read something like the following:

"I obviously need help. I realize I don't have what it takes. I can will it, but I can't do it. I decide to do good, but I don't really do it; I decide not to do bad, but then I do it anyway. . . It happens so regularly it's predictable. The moment I decide to do good, sin is there to trip me up. . . ."
(Romans 7, TMB)

Notions of dodging responsibility, passing the buck, excusing my wrongs held no attraction. I *knew* what disobedience felt like, knew wrong-doing, wrong-thinking, wrong-fantasizing when it entered the neighborhood. Like a drug-detecting dog, my conscience picked up transgression's scent. The buck stopped with me.

During those days in Christian culture, few religious communities walked with their people through the mine fields of sexual brokenness. There were likely more caregivers available than we knew. But that was part of the problem. They were not known.

Occasionally through my overseas years a handful of struggling men surfaced, gravitated together for encouragement and prayer. I linked up with such a group for a season. The effort was commendable as far as it went. Yet, although we did not intend to purposefully avoid certain topics such as sexual purity — we did. Each of us lived in Africa where wild game abounded, yet we always managed to ignore the elephant in the room.

A day would eventually come when Missions agencies, church councils and team leaders would compassionately open doors that had been long shut. To counsel, to pray with the broken and their spouses.

However, many in Christian service simply did the best they could to forge ahead. Pretty much in silence, managing their demons. Some, myself included, muddled along for years. The Holy Spirit graciously watched over our wounded, transgressing, saved-yet-fractured souls. We mercifully made it through without falling as casualties. We brought with us some scars, yet still moved forward. Limping with rays of hope, our marriage companions were often our greatest source of strength.

For other men, their suffering goes on undisclosed even today. Their pain real, their wounds deep, shame binds them and replays a false narrative in their minds. . . *there is no place to turn.*

May these gain help. Through the divine *Friend.* Through His children, his wounded healers.

Like those I would one day find.

Chapter Forty-Seven

SWIFT AND DEEP

MEANWHILE, life moved forward. Joys and triumphs marked much of it with family and friends. With ministry, through dry and rainy seasons.

Had I known my dirt bike could have landed at the bottom of a river before day's end, I might have stayed in bed.

Rains had been falling off and on for several days around Suna Mission, punctuated from time to time with pummeling downpours. My *piki-piki* slipped and slithered beneath me for miles along the muddy roadway, finally bringing me to a bridge. Submerged beneath a torrent of waters.

It was the bridge I planned to cross which would take me to Lake Victoria's shoreline. I was slated to preach the Sunday service in a fishing village.

Great volumes of murky brown raced along, a steady, turbulent surge passing both under and above the concrete bridge. Slowing the bike to a halt I let my feet find the muddy road surface. I sat some moments just taking in the scene. A young Luo man approached as I dismounted.

Smiling cheerily, he wasted no time offering me a proposition once the customary greetings were out of the way.

"Would you like to go over to the other side?" He hardly took a breath before adding, "I can get you there. . . ." The youth quickly surveyed the Suzuki and waved an open palm toward it before concluding, "and your *piki-piki,* too!"

Shy of any strong conviction to leap at his offer, I questioned what he had in mind.

"Come. Just come."

I clambered behind him up a muddy hill, a rise from which we could now take in more of the river upstream. I wasn't quite ready for the view.

At the water's edge lay a home-built canoe, long and narrow. It had been wrestled to shore and held in place by two captains. Into the canoe was lifted a hefty bag of maize, probably a good 70 pounds worth. What most caught my eye was an animal being drawn, much against its will, down the steep bank to the canoe.

"*Kuja! Kuja!* (Come! Come!)," shouted the man who leveraged the donkey's makeshift harness. His comrade energetically shoved from the animal's backside. The poor creature's resistance proved futile as it skidded nearer and nearer its watery destination.

The donkey's handler passed the harness rope to the nearest boats-man who made sure the animal went into the water alongside the vessel rather than *into it.*

Once the craft was loaded, off they rowed. The donkey swam nervously alongside, its jaw held taut by the keeper. Now and then, it bumped against the canoe's side.

Whatever was true about the action-laced drama, the mariner's labors convinced me. To entrust my old dirt bike to them. With one condition.

"Not a single scratch must be added to the bike until it's safely across and sitting on the opposite bank."

If this feat was met satisfactorily, I would add an extra two Kenyan shillings on the agreed fare. I wasn't so concerned about added dings to the already-scarred machine. I simply wished to make the strong point that neither the Suzuki nor myself landed at the bottom of the river.

Two additional canoes made their way to our shore. I struggled to keep my balance on the steep, sloshy terrain.

Twenty minutes later and a good way farther down-stream, both my *piki-piki* and me alighted intact on the oppo-site shore. Balancing in the canoe, I had snapped a picture of the bike. Its 250-cc frame was held perfectly upright by two strapping Luo youth. The photo made next month's news-letter, its caption advising, "watch and pray."

Chapter Forty-Eight

THE AFRICAN WAY

"YOU WILL SLEEP at my house tonight." The stranger pointed to a thatched dwelling in the distance. His words came more as factual statement than invitation.

The high school boy emerged as I straddled my motorbike atop the gravel road not far from Africa's largest lake. Daylight had faded. My bike's head-lamp struggled to project its beam outward through an increasing mist.

At least I'm not awash in a downpour. Not yet.

Once the drizzle began, I brought the *pikipiki* to a stop. I knew I was in for a long, perhaps soaking, ride the remaining fifty miles. The bike had been through a lot since leaving Nyabisawa Mission early that morning. It bounced and slipped, zigzagging ruts carved from cattle tracks and rivulets of earlier rains.

The boy's first greeting framed a question, "Hello, sir. My name is Joseph. Where are you going?"

"Hello Joseph. I'm Jerry. Taking the long way to Nyabi-sawa. Going home."

"But sir," his voice grew solemn, "you do not want to

travel this way at night. The next village ahead is Rodi. Bad people are there these days. When you pass through, they will throw stones at you. It is not a safe place to pass."

Reaching forward to wipe gathering moisture from the head lamp, I pondered the revelation. The schoolboy turned and with the wave of a hand indicated a trio of grass-roofed huts not far off the road. Night was descending and in equatorial Africa the shift from light to dark occurs in a heartbeat.

"You will sleep at my house tonight."

Once the *pikipiki* was secured inside the largest hut, I followed my young host to an impromptu sleeping quarter. It felt as if I had stepped onto the center of an open National Geographic magazine. African bush-country. Circular hut. Thatch roof. Floor of hardened earth smooth and clean-swept.

"I will stay out here in this room," Joseph announced. I glanced about as we passed through. Except for a sisal mat rolled up at the far wall, the room was bare.

"The house is my mother's. She is the second wife of my father. She is not here tonight."

We passed through an opening into the hut's only other room. It was small, the area barely allowing for a single, narrow cot. The light of his kerosene lantern revealed the cot's neatly-tucked bedding and a navy-blue blanket. A mosquito net, suspended from the roof, draped the bed. The net appeared adequate to keep any malaria-laden pests at a distance.

This small side-room and mosquito-shielded bed normally served the high-schooler as his own sleeping space. Nothing I said could persuade him to assign me the other room and the floor mat. This was the African way with guests.

I wonder how Ann's doing? Wish I had a way of being in touch.

A generous nighttime meal in the main hut with my young host and his family ensured deep, restful sleep.

Stirred awake next morning by a string of rooster crows, I emerged from the mosquito netting. I bundled it above the bed in a loose knot, then joined Joseph for bread and sweet hot tea that smelled slightly of charcoal embers. I thanked all the family, pulled on my helmet and was on my way. The last image was through my rear-view mirror. Joseph, with a white-toothed smile gleaming from his ebony Luo face, waved a vigorous farewell.

I passed through Rodi without incident, no rowdy mischief-makers, no stones to dodge.

Quite a weekend. Traversing a swollen river, my bike and me, aboard makeshift canoes. Preaching and fellowshipping at a Lake Victoria village. Hosted and dined overnight in a home, where hospitality rivaled the best of Kenya's tourist hotels.

In the pre-cell-phone days of Africa's 1970s, my wife chose to adopt a new practice.

"Jerry, if you're out in remote places and you don't make it back when expected and if I don't hear from you. . . well, I just won't worry. It's Africa. I'll pray and trust you're fine."

Chapter Forty-Nine

BEYOND WORDS

SOMETIMES SPOKEN ACCOUNTS of unthinkable wrongs get rejected outright by the listener's mind. Like a defense mechanism, the brain discards what is too painful, too dreadful to take in.

"They put my crying newborn there. Outside there. For the wild dogs or the hyenas to do as they would."

The poised tribal woman re-living her account was in her forties. She sat nearly immobile — her thoughts, even her body, seemingly lost in another time. Perhaps some things are better left behind. "I came to live in this area, several bus rides from my own people."

She had been brought here, far from her family's region to the north, an outsider bride to a local tribesman. Her native clan followed their own practices, some good, others less so. What her own people did not practice was infanticide.

"The clan into which I married had beliefs about child-bearing. Superstitions, I think." Grace's words fell with little emotion. The days of jagged pain tearing at her mother heart had long past. But the memory lived fresh.

"If twins were born to a home, it was a bad sign, a bad omen."

One of the two babies would be let go, Grace told us. Outside the hut, at nightfall. Outside, where hungry creatures scavenged for dinner.

"When the time for a baby like mine should come, it must be let go."

Could this be real? I had heard of pagan practices in far off places. *Was I truly living in such a place?*

The African woman spoke of the occasional baby, like her firstborn, whose only wrong was failing to make her arrival to the world head-first. A breach presentation.

Those years ago, her labor pains reached what seemed their limit. She strained a final time. Moments passed. A wave of relief. Cries of a newborn — vibrant, healthy-sounding cries.

But not cries to be celebrated.

The new mother helplessly agonized as her mother-in-law moved the baby out of reach, then beyond the dwelling's entrance, out into the night.

As my wife and I learned the story, we were taken by the nearness of it. The loss of this newborn happened just a few years prior to our reaching Kuria-land.

Mercifully for Grace, another pregnancy followed and later, another still. Each pregnancy heralded entries into the world of children lucky enough to arrive in acceptable fashion. Along the way Grace entrusted her life to Christ, and grew into a beloved leader among women, a matriarch of the faith.

Chapter Fifty

INSIDE INFORMATION

DOES the presence of foreign missionaries matter? Does their coming really bring a difference? And what about the nationals, laboring with them now as co-equals. . . do they supply a perspective?

I found through the years I had made my home in the company of unheralded heroes, humble messengers declaring a scandalous gospel.

The earlier questions were being answered. . .

"Disgraceful."

The Cessna 206 hummed through the skies over Tanzania's highlands as the female passenger, strapped securely in her seat adjacent the pilot, resumed her complaint.

"Missionary groups should just stay away. Stop meddling. Stop interfering with the beautiful traditions of cultures not their own. They have no right."

My pilot friend, Denny, had recounted to me visits he sometimes witnessed among his passengers, as they soared above the African plain. This time he was ferrying a European businesswoman to a Tanzania destination. Mission aviation groups sometimes assisted non-religious personnel. Denny's passenger spoke with a German accent, and she was on a roll.

"Why do they feel they must meddle? Why not leave the tribal groups alone, to their own rich customs? The arrogance of it! Peddling their religious message where it is not needed."

In the plane's rear seat sat Daniel, an African, tall and slender. He was Maasai by tribe, mentor to young evangelists, a churchman. Daniel listened to the woman, silent, attentive. When he sensed she'd finished her commentary, he leaned forward.

"I am sorry, madam, may I ask your view of something?"

She tilted her head.

Daniel's respectful tone continued. "Please help me with this. I have been hearing your complaint. My thought is to do with my own people in the region here.

"When missionaries came, they found us with many problems. We suffered diseases which shortened our lives. Our people had not known what brought some of the sicknesses or how to treat them.

"Our people of an earlier time lacked knowledge of other things. We could not read books. Our understanding stayed small.

"Then visitors began arriving, coming to us from Europe, from America. With them they brought things like medicines. They started clinics and began showing us about our sicknesses, their causes. Our conditions began improving.

"These people seemed to care about us. Books came. Teachers brought literacy to my people. Schools were built. Our lives were changing."

The aircraft continued her path through the skies. Daniel's

voice was strong and steady, competing with the engine's steady hum.

"And, madam, we were a fearful people. We have always felt there is a spirit world —invisible among the people and our tribes, but real. This fear came from troubling forces. We mostly feared death.

"Then the visitors, these missionaries, brought to us another message. They showed us about God.

"My question is this one, please. Are you saying those missionary people should not have left their places and come to us? With their medicines and their schools and the news to help us with our fear?"

Daniel had spoken in a respectful, reasoning way. He and the pilot awaited the visitor's response.

An airstrip came into view.

The plane began its descent, then landed. In silence.

Chapter Fifty-One

A SACRED HUSH

OUR MOVE from Kenya to Tanzania came fifteen years after our first landing in Africa. Ann and I felt we had grown in a variety of ways.

"Africa is a fruitful land," I laughed with tribespeople. "When my wife and I came, we were two. Now we are five!"

This country and her people had changed us, bringing to our souls more treasure than we had brought them. I savored mental images of individuals — Kenyans without whose presence would have left me less a man — people such as my friend, Nashon.

In the African savannah where acacia trees with their alluring, flat-topped forms dot the landscape, an adolescent boy was cornered by cattle thieves. The boy, a simple herdsman, made a futile attempt to seek refuge among his father's herd of semi-nourished cows. Horrifying moments raced like short distance sprinters toward the finish tape. The boy was seized and beaten, his life taken by the neighboring tribal warriors.

Heartless. Senseless. In the worldview of the tribesmen,

however, there was *nothing* senseless about their deed. For generations nomadic lore dictated that all cattle were created by God as a gift. Any means to retrieve what was rightfully theirs was deemed acceptable. The "retrieving of cattle" was a kind of calling.

Pastor Nashon was alerted of his young brother's death by the high-pitched wailing of nearby village women. Through grapevine media common to rural Africa, word of the tragedy reached our mission station several miles to the west.

Mounting my orange and aging dirt-bike, I ran my helmet strap through the cinch ring and secured it snugly beneath my chin.

A brief prayer, *Pastor Nashon needs a friend. Help me somehow be such a friend.*

Mindful of an inner tension, I tried to push back my growing sense of inadequacy. Comforting loved ones who've experienced the expected demise of an aged family member can be daunting enough. But this defied any category.

What would I say once my *piki-piki* was brought to a dusty halt? How would I myself process such news? How could I console the grieving pastor whose brother's life had been so brutally taken?

◊◊◊

Nashon, a man barely my junior, gave a warm smile as he offered the Swahili greeting, "The Lord be praised." Though a common greeting among believers, the words seemed especially poignant.

I quietly entered the dirt-floor hut and took the seat offered. The flavor of charcoal-heated chai, its vapors loitering above a fresh-washed mug.

Nashon was a modest and gentle spiritual shepherd, entrusted with the care of a small Christian community. He had labored as pastor just under two years, this with little formal Bible training. But Nashon's heart was rooted in Christ's love and in his clear calling to serve.

We sipped our hot chai and spoke in a softer, more subdued manner. Finally, I rallied my best voice to offer comfort. This would not be easy.

In unusual irony, Nashon sympathized with me. His eyes conveyed brotherly care. He leaned forward in his simple, primitive-like chair. "Brother Jerry, I want to speak something."

My turn to lean in and listen.

Nashon paused, then continued, "I forgive those men who have done this thing. I forgave them, actually, once I learned of the sad event."

Was I hearing correctly? Not a trace of pretense belied his calm voice.

"I know these people do not understand what they have done. They do not know. They need Jesus, so I have begun praying for them that they should know him and gain his peace."

Listening to this humble shepherd-leader I was perplexed. I felt myself deeply moved. And I was suddenly aware of the presence of God.

Beneath the long grass weavings forming the roof of this Kuria home, I was seated in Solomon's temple of the living God. I sat next to Isaiah, trembling at heaven's voices crying *"Holy, Holy"* in the sanctuary. The earthen floor under my feet might have dictated with hushed voice that I remove my shoes.

A reversing of roles had occurred. The missionary-teacher had come to give comfort. But I sat voiceless as the young, ill-educated, nearly-impoverished pastor stepped to his invisible lectern.

Nashon's non-sermon to his audience of one conveyed with conviction the message of an ancient, extravagant grace. Radical forgiveness issued from one wholly taken by mercy.

The Lord be praised. Indeed.

Chapter Fifty-Two

BLUECOLLAR IMPRINT

1992, the year that changed everything, began with a pensive phone call. "I would like you here."

My father's voice broke slightly, then went quiet. I knew a transatlantic flight lay ahead.

At age 79, after decades inhaling industrial asbestos, the medical findings were grim. An aggressive cancer, mesothelioma, had attacked the lining about his lungs.

We had planned this year as a season for relocating to the U.S. Our conversations often turned that direction, "Scott is almost college-age and will, like his sister before him, become a U.S. resident. Our parents with their challenges. . . ."

Ann's mother in Montana was losing ground in her leukemia fight.

"And hon — like we've been feeling — maybe our stint in Africa, at least this one, is winding down."

Relocating would mean nine-year-old Amy saying goodbye to the only friends she knew. A move would not be easy. "Let's keep praying."

And now, my father's call, his barely-uttered plea. Sensing

his days were likely numbered, he wanted his youngest nearby, at least for a visit.

"Oklahoma's March winds are still cold, honey, keep your jacket near." Zipping my backpack shut, we moved to the car. The bus station lay minutes away.

"I'll call when I reach Nairobi, and again, once in the states."

We kissed goodbye.

◊◊◊

The Okmulgee-Tulsa trips – four times weekly for Dad's radiation – felt bittersweet. I treasured the times, even when little talk passed between us. The days of this titan figure, our family's five-foot-nine giant, were numbered. A momentary setback came during my March visit, "Well son, looks like St. Francis wants me to move in."

Seated on a vinyl-covered sofa by the hospital window, I reflected a moment, then cleared my throat.

"Dad, could I ask a favor?"

His raised hospital bed poised him to a near-upright position. He nodded. I brought my chair to the bedside.

"Dad, you remember those stories in the Old Testament, where a father would lay his hand on his son and say a blessing over him?" My father's mind had always been keen. He tracked with me now. I was thankful the room, with its chemically-sterile odor, remained quiet, apart from the monitor's occasional beep-beep.

"It would mean a lot to me if you'd be willing to do that, give me your blessing now. . . here. No need to worry about right words. Do you think you could do that?"

His response was the kind he might have given a

construction supervisor, to update him on a blueprint. Certain. Without delay. "Yes. Sure, son."

Weathered plumber's hands rested atop my head. The blessing delivered did not come polished or flowery. Its eloquence lay in the straightforward language. Practical, commending me to the Lord's care. That God's counsel would come to a willing mind, that I pay attention to sensible guidance. The blessing was simple and sincere, a blue-collar benediction, stretching to maybe a minute. Moving the few steps back to the couch I was again reflective.

Savor these moments. They'll count among the richest of your lifetime.

Chapter Fifty-Three

HORIZON

WHAT'S in store for our future, our next step?

It was a periodic musing through the years, sometimes signaling a new direction, new location, new focus. Our time to leave Africa seemed rapidly nearing.

As I buckled in, I pondered family. The flight attendant clicked a mic and began her drill. Tanzania and home lay ahead. I was ready. Wonderings resumed.

How long will Dad be with us? Will I see him four months from now when we re-enter the U.S.? What about Mary, Ann's mom. . . when does she fight her last leukemia bout?

Amy would soon turn nine — African friends and places all she's known. Her two siblings, navigating culture in the land of their parents.

What of Ann and me? With years spent away from our motherland, how will that work? Even if for a season.

Made in the USA
Middletown, DE
16 August 2019